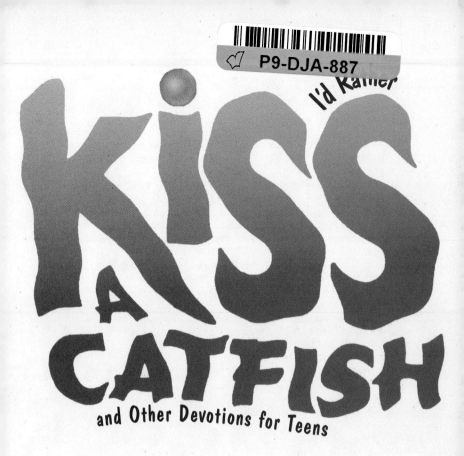

I'd Rather

KiSS
A
CATFISH

and Other Devotions for Teens

Karl Haffner

REVIEW AND HERALD® PUBLISHING ASSOCIATION
HAGERSTOWN, MD 21740

The author assumes full responsibility for the accuracy of all
facts and quotations as cited in this book.

Except where otherwise noted, Bible texts in this book are from the *Holy Bible,
New International Version.* Copyright © 1973, 1978, 1984, International Bible Society.
Used by permission of Zondervan Bible Publishers.
Scriptures credited to EB are quoted from *The Everyday Bible, New Century
Version,* copyright © 1987, 1988 by Word Publishing, Dallas, Texas 75039. Used by
permission.
Scriptures credited to ICB are quoted from the *International Children's Bible,
New Century Version,* copyright © 1983, 1986, 1988 by Word Publishing, Dallas,
Texas 75039. Used by permission.
Scriptures marked Message are from *The Message.* Copyright © 1993. Used by
permission of NavPress Publishing Group.
Bible texts credited to RSV are from the Revised Standard Version of the Bible,
copyright © 1946, 1952, 1971, by the Division of Christian Education of the National
Council of the Churches of Christ in the U.S.A. Used by permission.
Bible texts credited to TEV are from the *Good News Bible*—Old Testament:
Copyright © American Bible Society 1976; New Testament: Copyright © American
Bible Society 1966, 1971, 1976.
Verses marked TLB are taken from *The Living Bible,* copyright © 1971 by Tyndale
House Publishers, Wheaton, Ill. Used by permission.
Anecdotes in this volume are based on fact; however, in some instances details
have been changed to protect identities.

This book was
Edited by Gerald Wheeler
Designed by De Laine Mayden
Cover illustration by Chad Frye
Inside illustrations by Jim Paxton
Typeset: 12/13.5 Optima

PRINTED IN U.S.A.

00 99 98 97 96   10 9 8 7 6 5 4 3 2 1

R&H Cataloging Service
Haffner, Karl Mark, 1961-
    I'd rather kiss a catfish and other devotions for
teens.

    1. Teenagers—Prayer books and devotionals—
English.

242.63

ISBN 0-8280-1091-9

Dedication
to My Parents

To dad and mom, Cliff and Barbara Haffner . . .
Had I been you with a son like me, I'd have
packed my kid's lunch in a road map.

Instead, you loved me even when I broke
Randy's arm; stole the Weavers' tithe money; set
the garage on fire . . . I won't pain you with all the
memories. I'll simply say, "Thanks for showing
me what the gospel is all about."

I love you!

To My Father-in-law,
Clarence Gruesbeck...

You are the Gospel with skin on it. As my
seminary professor, my mentor in ministry, or my
Scrabble challenger, you're the best advertisement for the gospel that I've seen (although I still
contend that you had entirely too much fun
watching me squirm when I asked to marry your
daughter!).

Acknowledgments

Special thanks to:

Lori Peckham

Tim Lale

Chris Blake

Randy Fishell

Jeannette Johnson

If you don't like the way I write—blame them! They are the editors who have coaxed, trained, pruned, and encouraged me through many of the articles included in this volume. Like skilled surgeons, they have cut and cut and cut—until the words are strong and the meaning is clear.

Lori, thanks for introducing me to the world of writing. Your invitation to "try writing an article for our Thanksgiving issue" has dramatically altered my life. Without you I'd have no clue what malapropisms, sentence fragments, and split infinitives are all about. (I *still* don't understand the split infinitives!)

To the editors who make my scrambled thoughts make sense, thanks. Without you I'd be lost in a world of run-on sentences and misplaced capitals.

Contents

Contents, continuod

The Gospel

The Heart of the Matter

I felt like a rag doll in the dryer's spin cycle. Desperate to feel better, I made an appointment with Dr. Law.

"It's your heart," Dr. Law growled with the compassion of a bulldog.

"My heart?" I questioned. "There's no trace of heart trouble in my family. At least examine me."

"No diagnosis necessary," he snapped. "It's your heart."

"My heart has never given me problems. But my feet—oh boy, there's the problem! They have taken me to liquor stores and nightclubs and . . ."

"It's your heart."

"Doctor, please check out my hands. These lousy, dysfunctional hands have rolled dice, played cards, filled mugs with beer. Here's the problem," I insisted.

"It's not your hands; it's your heart."

"At least examine my ears. They have listened to dirty jokes and gossip and profanity and enough rock and roll to kill the Rolling Stones."

"It's your heart."

"There's plenty of other doctors in this city!" I stormed

out of his office like a stuntman from a cannon.

For the next 10 months I bounced from doctor to doctor to doctor—faithfully performing every prescription, yet never feeling healthy. Dr. Religion prescribed a regimen of baptism, church attendance, and tithing. Dr. Diet blamed my eating habits and suggested a menu of tofu, tree bark, and Garden Burgers. Dr. B. Good stripped my rings and bracelet off me and helped me stop going to movies.

While every doctor promised a cure, nothing could quiet the gnawing emptiness that ached within. In despair I returned to Dr. Law.

"It's your heart" were his first words. He hadn't changed his diagnosis.

"Yeah, yeah," I barked. "So what do I do?"

"You need a heart transplant."

"Glad it's nothing serious." My cynicism leaked like poison.

"Heart transplant or death." His words cut like a scalpel.

"OK, I'll let you do the operation."

"Oh, I don't operate," Dr. Law replied. "That's what I have a partner for. Follow me."

He led me across the hall to Dr. Grace's office.

"Are you ready for the operation?" Dr. Grace asked kindly.

"I, um, ah, I, ah . . ."

"Relax. I have never lost a case."

"OK, but give me a double dose of anesthetic."

"Oh no," he chuckled. "I want you awake for this so you can tell others about it."

Even my toenails sweat as he made the first incision. Suddenly the odor of a symphony of skunks filled the room.

"Peeeeeeee-yeeeeeeeeew." I grabbed a pillow to breathe through. "What is that disgusting smell?"

"It's your heart."

"My heart?"

"You can smell the dirty jokes and the gossip and the pornography—they've all collected here in your heart."

"I guess I really do need a new heart. By the way, what does a heart cost these days? I haven't seen any heart sales lately."

"Twenty-six million dollars," he said without looking up.

"Twenty-six million dol—um, ah, at 50 bucks a month, how long will this take to pay for?"

"You'll never pay for it," he laughed. "A Friend has taken care of it for you." Making his final stitch, Dr. Grace looked up. "There, how does that feel?"

"I feel better already," I said.

"You'll feel even better with exercise."

"Exercise?"

"Dr. Law and I are firm believers in exercise."

"Like what other doctors prescribed?"

"In a sense," Dr. Grace said. "Exercise is critical, but only after you have addressed the heart of the matter—which is a matter of the heart."

My mind swirled like a tornado. "About the Friend who paid for my new heart—um, could I, ah, meet Him?"

"Most certainly," Dr. Grace smiled. "Oh, but be prepared. In order to give you a new heart, His was crushed. So don't be surprised by the ugly, gaping scar in His side."

"God made him who had no sin to be sin for us, so that in him we might become the righteousness of God"
(2 Cor. 5:21).

Drugs, Sex, Harleys —and Grapes

Gangs, drugs, booze, and tattoos—Mr. Rice's testimony had all the elements to make any fifth grader pant with envy. Fresh off the streets and into the classroom, Mr. Rice would say, "I'm not proud of this, but I ran with the meanest gangs in Phoenix. In my old neighborhood the most popular form of transportation was the stretcher. The local gun shop had a back-to-school sale. The school song was a police siren. And we were all honor students —'yes, Your Honor . . . no, Your Honor . . .'"

As the story unfolded before wide-eyed fifth graders, Mr. Rice eventually came to the part about collapsing on the cold cement slab in reform school, surrendering his life to Jesus. That's when God called him to teach and minister to street kids like him.

In my mind nobody ranked as cool as Mr. Rice. He even preferred we call him "Bob" outside the classroom. Toooooo cool! He took us for airplane rides (sometimes he'd even skydive for us), horseback trips (he could always get his horse to rear up on its back two legs), and ice-cream stops (one time we packed 13 kids into his Opal to get there). He'd wrestle the whole class of 31 kids—and win. Occasionally he'd interrupt history class with "Bag this! Let's plaaaaaaaaaaaaaaaaaaaay ball!" And every other Thursday we'd stay over at Cedar Brook School to help Mr. Rice host a program for inner-city street kids.

It was the Thursday evenings that got to me. After the

final verse of "Kum by Yah," Mr. Rice would lay down his guitar and share his story: "I'm not proud of this . . ." Even the gangsters sat like statues in shock as he shared.

As I listened to his story, a curious feeling swallowed me. It was envy. You see, I didn't have a story—at least not one that anybody cared to hear. At the tender age of 6 I knelt at family worship and asked God to cleanse me of things such as spitting on my sister, stealing grapes at Harry's Market, and making a ruckus in church. *What good is a sissy testimony like that?* I asked myself.

So I wrote a new one. I planned to turn it in for extra-credit in hopes that Mr. Rice would read it as worship for the street kids.

"I'm not proud of this," I scribbled in my 10-year-old handwriting, "but last summer I blew $50,000 that I made dealing drugs." The opener was sure to evoke gasps from even the hardest criminals. "I guess I got into the wrong crowd. It all started with a bottle of glue. My girlfriend and I were having problems communicating. My parents were hassling me about my long hair. And my pet gerbil died. What was there to live for? So I went into my closet and popped the cap off a bottle of glue. I inhaled the dangerous fumes until the clothes hangers started telling me dirty jokes. I knew right then I was destined to hell because I couldn't stop laughing at the raunchy riddles. Sin had its grip on me, and I enjoyed it too much to let go.

"One thing led to another until I hooked up with mobster Antonio DaVincionio and found myself head-deep in the underworld of drugs, sex, money, and Harley-Davidsons. That's when I saw a funny-looking guy behind the goalpost at a football game holding a sign with John 3:16 on it. I vaguely remembered the text from my childhood, but when I looked it up again, it hit me—

God so loved Karl Haffner that He sent His Son to die for my sins. I asked forgiveness right then and committed my life to teaching kids like me who had gone astray."

The gripping testimony was ready to go public. But not before my mom discovered it under my pillow. "What's this all about?" she demanded.

"I, um, well, ah, I wanted to write up my story of how I found Jesus—you know, like my testimony."

"This is *your* testimony?"

"Well, yeah. Sure it is. It surprised you, didn't it? I've kept the secret real good, but it's time to come clean."

"This is your *true* testimony?" she pushed.

"Um, ah, yeah. You know it's true—at least the part about my gerbil dying."

Mom gently explained that sometimes little boys whose worst sins were committed at Harry's Market are the worst sinners of all. They're the ones who don't realize how sinful they are. She said whether it's stealing grapes or dealing drugs, we all deserve hell.

My mother reminded me of how Mr. Rice would always share in his testimony that it's only by Jesus' grace that he was saved. And it's only by Jesus' grace that Karl Haffner will be saved.

"Your testimony," she concluded, "isn't about what you have done. It's about what Jesus has done. And that is the most amazing story you could ever tell."

"For it is by grace you have been saved, through faith—and this not from yourselves, it is the gift of God— not by works, so that no one can boast" (Eph. 2:8, 9).

You Might Be a Spiritual Redneck If . . .

Jeff Foxworthy has tickled America's funny bone with his wacky guidelines to test whether you're a redneck. He claims you may be a redneck, if . . .
- You think the stock market has a fence around it.
- You own a home that is mobile and five cars that aren't.
- You pick your teeth from a catalog.
- Your wife has ever said, "Come move this transmission so I can take a bath."

With apologies to Mr. Foxworthy, I've started my own test for spiritual rednecks. I call them legalists. How do you fare in the redneck department?

You may be a legalist if . . .
- You use a stopwatch in your devotions.
- You make your toddler file a 1040 to report the quarter she found in the sofa.
- You think grace is the name of a perfume.
- Your checks feature eschatology charts.
- You think Morris Venden is a cat.
- Your license plate reads: UR24GOJOY
- You share your church attendance records at family reunions.
- You have a party and your neighbors don't even realize it.
- Your translation of Matthew 5:5 is "Only people like me will inherit the earth."

- You call the police to report someone refilling his Big Gulp after sipping it.
- You set your watch in church to beep at 12:00 noon.
- Your key chain is a life-sized replica of the Ten Commandments.
- You count the number of groceries in the lady's cart in front of you when you're in the express lane.
- You stare at a can of frozen apple juice because it says "Concentrate."
- You have a lie detector in your house.
- Any of your hobbies require commentaries.
- Your parrot can say, "It's not sundown yet."

"All over the world this gospel is bearing fruit and growing, just as it has been doing among you since the day you heard it and understood God's grace in all its truth" (Col. 1:6).

"If" and "Always"

Perhaps the biggest word in Scripture is that two-letter one, *if*.

"*If* we confess our sins, he is faithful and just and will forgive us our sins and purify us from all unrighteousness" (1 John 1:9). Confessing sins—admitting failure—isn't easy.

"I cheated on my algebra final."

"I am addicted to pornography, and I need help."

"I'm sorry that in my rage I hit you."

"I've been cheating on my girlfriend."

"I am an alcoholic."

"I failed to defend you when I knew it was malicious gossip."

Oddly enough, Jesus taught that confession is the pathway to joy. "Happy are the people," he said, "who know they are in trouble and have enough sense to admit it" (Matt. 5:3, 4, paraphrased).

Of all the paths to joy, this has to be the most peculiar. To think that true satisfaction begins with deep sadness—odd, isn't it?

Odder still is the fact that God is always faithful to respond to our confessions with grace—with unearned forgiveness and love. *Always.*

Ask any of Scripture's hall-of-famers, and they will confirm—*always*. Ask Noah if God will forgive a drunk. Ask Abraham if God will forgive a man who sacrificed his wife's chastity because of his own cowardice. Ask Moses if God will forgive a murderer. Ask David how God responds to a man who jumps into bed with the next-door neighbor. Ask Jeremiah if God will forgive a whiner.

I'd Rather Kiss a Catfish

Ask any of the saints about God's response to our confessions, and they will answer, "Always."

Always faithful.

Always just.

Always forgiving.

That's the promise of 1 John 1:9. But don't ignore the premise: *if.*

If we confess. There's that gnarly two-letter word again. The premise upon which the promise hinges—*if.*

Believe me when I say that nothing is more satisfying than the peace of confession. And nothing is more certain than the pardon of Christ.

So what confessions do you need to make? What past sins are choking the joy out of your life? What tentacles of guilt are squeezing the zip out of your Christian walk? What is keeping you from joy?

Perhaps such joy is only a two-letter word away.

Passing the Final

Steve Winger tells of his last college test—a final in a logic class known for its difficult exams. Anticipating that terrible day of judgment made students sweat bile.

"To help us on our test, the professor told us we could bring as much information to the exam as we could fit on a piece of notebook paper. Most students crammed as many facts as possible on the 8½" x 11" sheet of paper," Steve recalls.

"But one student walked into class, put a piece of notebook paper on the floor, and had an advanced logic student stand on the paper. The advanced logic student told him everything he needed to know. He was the only student to receive an A."

We too face a terrible day of judgment. Are you prepared?

"What?"

Some believe being prepared means cramming on the "what" questions. *What* day should we worship on? *What* meats are clean and unclean? *What* happens after a person dies?

"When?"

Others concoct charts and graphs and focus on the "when" questions. *When* will the exam take place? *When* will it occur in relation to the millennium? *When* will the day of probation occur?

"How?"

Still others insist on addressing the "how" questions. *How* are we saved—through faith or works? *How* can we prove we are the remnant? *How* will we survive the time of trouble?

"Who?"

As important as these questions seem, they are as worthless as a calculator with dead batteries when it comes to the final exam. Cram your cheat sheet with enough facts to boggle Einstein, and you'll still be found wanting on the day of judgment. You may be as meek as Moses, as smart as Solomon, and as prolific as Paul, and still be lost.

For salvation comes not in knowing what or when or how—but who. Only those who have focused on the "who" question will find grace in the judgment. For they know Someone who will stand in their place.

**"Salvation is found in no one else,
for there is no other name under heaven
given to men by which we must be saved"
(Acts 4:12).**

Perspectives on Grace

"When Jesus went home, He left the front door open."—Max Lucado.

"If His conditions are met, God is bound by His Word to forgive any man or any woman of any sin because of Christ."—Billy Graham.

"But God demonstrates his own love for us in this: While we were still sinners, Christ died for us." Romans 5:8.

"If God can't save Jeffrey Dahmer, then He can't save you or me."—Chuck Colson.

"Years ago in the South there was a boy who wanted to join a church. So the deacons began examining him. They asked, 'How did you get saved?' His answer was 'God did His part, and I did my part.' They thought there was something wrong with his doctrine, so they questioned further, 'What was God's part, and what was your part?' His explanation was a good one. He said, 'God's part was the saving, and my part was the sinning. I done run from Him as fast as my sinful heart and rebellious legs could take me. He done took out after me till He run me down.' My friend, that is the way I got saved also."—J. Vernon McGee.

"In him we have redemption through his blood, the forgiveness of sins, in accordance with the riches of God's grace that he lavished on us with all wisdom and understanding."—Ephesians 1:7.

"The New Testament proclaims that at some unforeseeable time in the future God will bring down the final curtain on history, and there will come a day on which all our days and all the judgments upon us and all our judgments upon each other will themselves be judged. The judge will be Christ. In other words, the one who judges us most finally will be the one who loves us most fully."—Frederick Buechner.

"A man can no more take in a supply of grace for the future than he can eat enough today to last him for the next six months, nor can he inhale sufficient air into his lungs with one breath to sustain life for a week to come. We are permitted to draw upon God's store of grace from day to day as we need it."— D. L. Moody.

"As the earth can produce nothing unless it is fertilized by the sun, so we can do nothing without the grace of God."—John Vianney.

The Gospel
According to Bloopers

 Failure Vitamins

You pick the sport and I'll fail at it—*really* fail! Even a sport as simple as golf (that's flog spelled backward) provides me endless opportunities for bloopers.

Fortunately, the pro in the golf shop didn't understand my affinity for failure and sports. "If you boys will hurry," he said, "you can tee off before the senior citizens' tournament. Just keep up the pace."

We raced to the first tee. I addressed the ball, ready to blast that Top-Flite straight down the fairway.

Then I glanced behind me. Fifty old men who appeared to be dressed in polyester shower curtains glared at me. They hushed their chattering.

Silence.

I reviewed the basics in my mind. *Keep your head down. Flex your knees. Swing easy. Snap your wrists through the ball. Uncork your hips.*

I whacked the ball, slicing it low and hard. Rather than sailing down the fairway, however, it smacked straight into the women's tee and ricocheted past the men standing behind me—triggering their pacemakers into red alert.

The ball sailed into the garage under the clubhouse where a white Cadillac Coupe Deville was parked. *Clatter! Crash! Bang!*

"Don't think you can play it from in there," one aged man (who almost lost his toupee to my misguided missile) smirked.

"Don't sweat it," another man giggled. "Here, son, give it another shot." He tossed me a new ball.

I launched his ball, but this time it landed smack in the center of the fairway! The gallery of senior citizens applauded—my perfect throw!

Failure is the one thing I'm really good at—not only in sports but in life! Perhaps you are too.

Failure is spreading gossip you regret, or compromising your integrity, or caving in to the same old sin. Failure is the feeling of being paralyzed by lurid thoughts. It's snubbing God—again.

Since I am so good at failure, I treasure my spiritual medicine cabinet of "Failure Vitamins." One of my favorite vitamins is Psalm 73:26: "My flesh and my heart may fail, but God is the strength of my heart and my portion forever."

I think of it as God's way of tossing me a new ball to try again.

 Consider This

B. C. Forbes once said, "History has demonstrated that the most notable winners usually encountered heartbreaking obstacles before they triumphed. They won because they refused to become discouraged by their defeats."

Consider this:

When Lucille Ball began studying to be an actress in 1927, the head instructor of the John Murray Anderson Drama School told her, "Try any other profession. Any other."

In 1959 a Universal Pictures executive dismissed Clint Eastwood and Burt Reynolds at the same meeting with the following statements: To Burt Reynolds: "You have no talent." To Clint Eastwood: "You have a chip on your tooth, your Adam's apple sticks out too far, and you talk too slow."

Malcolm Forbes, the late editor in chief of *Forbes* magazine, one of the most successful business publications in the world, failed to make the staff of the school newspaper when he was an undergraduate at Princeton University.

Louis L'Amour, successful author of more than 100 Western novels with more than 200 million copies in print, received 350 rejections before he made his first sale. He later became the first American novelist to receive a special congressional gold medal in recognition of his distinguished career as an author and contributor to the nation through his historically based works.

Wilma Rudolph was the twentieth of 22 children. Born prematurely, her survival was doubtful. When she was 4 years old she contracted double pneumonia and scarlet fever, which left her with a paralyzed left leg. At age 9 she removed the metal leg brace she had been dependent on and began to walk without it. By 13 she had developed a rhythmic walk, which doctors said was a miracle. That same year she decided to become a runner. She entered a race and came in last. For the next few years every race she entered, she came in last. Everyone told her to quit, but she kept running. One day she actually won a race. And then another. From then on she won every race she entered. Eventually this little girl, who was told she would never walk again, went on to win three Olympic gold medals.

Wilma Rudolph once said, "My mother taught me very early to believe I could achieve any accomplishment I wanted to. The first was to walk without braces."

"He gives strength to the weary and increases the power of the weak" (Isa. 40:29).

I Am Joe's Conscience

...nnoying as screeching nails on a chalk
board. Or I can be as soothing as a gurgling brook in the
mountains. I am Joe's conscience.

Before I tell you about myself, however, let me de-
scribe Joe. Joe is a sophomore at Bellevue Christian High.
He likes the Orlando Magic, snowboarding, peanut
M&M's, and girls. And girls. And girls.

Joe has the physique of a music stand—big head, big
feet, and a body that's hardly noticeable. He wears
glasses and flashes a magnetic smile (he wears braces).
His dad's an engineer, and his mom works part-time as a
legal secretary. Joe's your basic kid just trying to survive
the terror of immortal zits, two sisters, and a world history
teacher named Mrs. Grummstead.

Now I'll tell you about myself. I live in a mess—the
east side estates of Joe's brain—and work out of my home
as a delivery boy disbursing messages all around the
body. My hobbies include jogging around memory lane
and serving as president of the ethical debate team. My
nicknames include "a little voice," "the devil," and
"something within me." But most people just call me
Joe's conscience.

Put to the Test

As a professional conscience I get to badger Joe
whenever he faces difficult decisions. Yesterday's world
history class is a good example.

It started the night before when Joe went to 7-Eleven
for a Super Big Gulp rather than studying about the
Industrial Revolution. Then he opted for reruns of *The*

Simpsons, a fight with his sister, and a game of Nintendo over reading about textile mills. Joe figured some cramming on the bus in the morning would suffice.

The cram session turned into a see-if-you-can-get-Amanda-to-giggle-at-touching-my-tongue-to-my-nose game. Actually it didn't matter because preparing for a Grummstead exam in 15 minutes would be like trying to eat a watermelon during a commercial break. The more information Joe tried to swallow, the messier it got, and when he scanned the test, I whispered, "You are in boiling nacho cheese now!"

"Oooooooh," Joe groaned, "why didn't I study?"

"I told you," I said. "Didn't I—"

"Quiet!"

"I told you! But no, you had to study Super Mario Brothers instead, and you had to watch idiot Homer—"

"Quiet!" he repeated.

But that's something I've never been good at. When Joe least wants to talk is when I get as stubborn as a Chevy 4x4 in mud. "If you had just skimmed the textbook, at least you'd get one answer correct."

"I'll get this first one," he said. "Let's see, name, that's easy—Joseph Montgomery. I'm on a roll."

"OK, Mr. IBM Brain, look at the next question. 'What year has Professor W. Rostow suggested as the beginning of the Industrial Revolution?' I don't think Bart mentioned it on his show last night."

Joe's forehead moistened like Shaquille O'Neal's head during a game. His eyes twitched. His left foot tapped.

He read the next question. And the next question. And the essay question. He could have been reading a philosophy book in Japanese—it would have made more sense.

Then someone who lives in a brain cell on the south side suggested, "Mellow out, Joe. Look to your left. Glenda

Cho isn't leaning over her paper."

"But um—" Joe weakly protested.

I could sense Joe wasn't listening. Often he pretends he doesn't hear or understand me.

Joe glanced to his left. Glenda was scribbling the answers faster than a doctor autographing a prescription.

"Better look now," the south side tempter whispered. "If you don't, Glenda will be on page 2, and you won't get any answers on the—"

"You look at her answers," I interrupted, "and I'll make you feel like you're sleeping on a porcupine tonight."

"Donkey feathers! Come on, Joe, you can sleep tonight. If Glenda didn't want you to check out her answers, she wouldn't be sitting like that."

"I'll be like sandpaper on your eyeball—"

"Come on, Joe, just this—"

"I'll be an ice pick from ear to ear."

"Come on! Hurry!"

"I'll—"

"Would—?"

Joe put his right hand on his forehead to disguise his glance. His eyes shifted left. His head cocked slightly.

Joe jotted down Glenda's answer: "1783." He peeked for the next answer.

"You know better," I hollered. My words echoed in his mind. A party broke out in the south side slums. All the commotion caused Joe's head to throb and his behind to fidget.

That night as Joe lay in bed he was as restless as a muzzled mouse in a cheese factory. As I'd promised, I tortured him. "You need to go to Mrs. Grummstead and confess . . . Do what is right . . . What would Jesus do? . . . How would you like to study hard and have a lazy scum copy your answers?" My taunting continued through the night and all through breakfast this morning.

As I write this, Joe is slouching in the back seat of the school bus. He is quiet and gazes out the window. Today he is not flirting with Amanda. I continue to jab him.

I'm not sure Joe will listen to me. Regardless of what he does, however, I won't get flustered. I'll keep working, because I know there are a lot more Joes where he came from.

"Let us draw near to God with a sincere heart in full assurance of faith, having our hearts sprinkled to cleanse us from a guilty conscience and having our bodies washed with pure water" (Heb. 10:22).

Once Upon an Accident

twisted in the

Seems a young fellow was driving home from school when he snagged the fender of his car on the bumper of another car. He was on the verge of tears because the car was his dad's prized possession, fresh out of the showroom. How was he ever going to explain the damage to his father?

The driver of the other car was sympathetic, but explained that they must note each other's license and registration numbers. As the young man reached into an envelope to retrieve the documents, a piece of paper fell out. In a heavy masculine scrawl were these words: "In case of an accident . . . remember, my boy, it's you I love, not the Buick!"

A story not too distant from our own. We too have bloopers aplenty. The biting words we should have swallowed. The party we'd avoid, given another chance.

But it's too late. We stand tangled in a pickle. Our poor choices have scratched and dented our lives. Now it's time for the consequences. It's time to face the Father.

So we grimace at the thought of coming clean. We wait for our just reward.

And that's when our Father's note flutters to the floor. "In case of bloopers . . . remember, child, it's you I love, not your behavior." Oh sure, the bills for our blunders still come due. And the tentacles of regret continue to embrace us. But isn't it reassuring to know our Father will always love us in spite of our bloopers? We can't crash bad enough to deter our Father's love! So go ahead. Show Him your banged-up life. The scuffs and scars won't offend Him. Instead, His scuffs and scars will cover yours. Remember, His specialty is loving the boy, not the behavior.

Now, *that's* a story worth retelling.

**"You forgave the iniquity of your people
and covered all their sins"
(Ps. 85:2).**

Pobody's Nerfoot

In a perfect world . . .

10. Dog owners would not kiss their pets on the mouth.
9. Everyone would listen to country music.
8. Oreo cookies would have the nutritional value of tofu.
7. Parents would never say "Because I said so."
6. You'd never get behind an indecisive family of eight in a drive-through.
5. Toilet seats would be heated.
4. Taxes would be optional.
3. Canker sores would taste like M&M's.
2. Your date would always order the value meal.
1. Algebra would be as riveting as an action movie.

Such would be a perfect world. But we don't live in a perfect world. You know why? Because you ain't perfect. And neither am I. That's the bad news.

The good news is God doesn't expect us to be perfect. He knows we won't achieve perfection until we get to heaven. He asks only that we daily strive to be more Christlike.

Mountain climbers who slip and slide a few feet don't pack it up and quit. They trudge forward, only now they know where not to put their feet.

When we slip and slide backward, we should accept God's forgiveness and move on, vowing not to walk that path again. Why should we be harder on ourselves than God is? He knows that anybody with a heartbeat on this old earth will be perfectly imperfect. Pobody's nerfect. If you can't tolerate the imperfect people who make mistakes, then I'd suggest you stop making them yourself!

"Repent, then, and turn to God, so that your sins may be wiped out, that times of refreshing may come from the Lord" (Acts 3:19).

 ## Perspectives on Failure

"The law tells me how crooked I am. Grace comes along and straightens me out."—Dwight L. Moody.

"The Lord's love never ends. His mercies never stop. They are new every morning. Lord, your loyalty is great."—Lamentations 3:22, 23, EB.

"Show me a thoroughly satisfied man—and I will show you a failure."— Thomas Edison.

"Failure is living without knowing what life is all about, feeding on things that do not satisfy, thinking you have everything, only to find out in the end you have nothing that matters."—*Author Unknown.*

Two bums were sitting leaning against a tree in the field. One said, "I'm sick and tired of this life. I'm sick and tired of sleeping in the cold and rain, begging for food, wearing torn clothes. I'm sick of it."
The second bum said, "If you feel like that, why don't you get a job?"
The first bum sat up and said, "And admit I'm a failure?"
"There is no failure so great that a Christian cannot rise from it."—Ellen G. White.

George Washington, alone and cold and discouraged at Valley Forge, penned these words to his favorite chaplain, Israel Evans: "It will ever be the first wish of my heart to aid your pious endeavors to inculcate a due sense of the dependence we ought to place in that all-wise and powerful Being on whom alone our success depends."

"Ninety-nine percent of the failure comes from people who have the habit of making excuses."—George Washington Carver.

"We shall often have to bow down and weep at the feet of Jesus because of our shortcomings and mistakes, but we are not to be discouraged. Even if we are overcome by the enemy, we are not cast off, not forsaken and rejected of God. No; Christ is at the right hand of God, who also maketh intercession for us."—Ellen G. White.

"We must not become tired of doing good. We will receive our harvest of eternal life at the right time. We must not give up."—Galatians 6:9, EB.

"Nature shouts of this beginning-again-God, this God who can make all our failures regenerative, the One who is God of risings again, who never tires of fresh starts, nativities, renaissances in persons or in culture. God is a God of starting over, of genesis and re-genesis. He composts life's sour fruits, moldering rank and decomposing; He applies the organic matter to our new day chances; He freshens the world with dew; He hydrates withered human hearts with his downpouring spirit."
—Karen Mains.

The Gospel
According to Clutter

Clutterly Disgusting

Recently I bought Ronni Eisenberg's book entitled
Organize Yourself!—but I misplaced it. I think I saw it
last near the heaps of boxes cluttering our garage. Since
we're in the middle of moving, our lives feel like a flea
market. OK, so "moving" is just an excuse—I felt swallowed by clutter long before we started packing.

How do we collect so much clutter? I cleaned my
garage yesterday and found 14 extension cords. Doesn't
that smack of dysfunctional to you? I could plug in a radio
in Seattle and take it to San Francisco without losing power.

Old running shoes line my garage wall. It's a personal
thing—I feel guilty throwing them away. How do you tell
a pair of Nikes that took you through the Emerald City
Marathon that you don't need them anymore? Shoes have
feelings too, you know.

And paint. I've got enough half-empty cans to coat
the Tower of Babel. Who knows when they may crank up
construction again and call me for supplies?

But when your garage looks like Hurricane Iniki and
Hurricane Andrew got married there, it's time to declare

"Clutter be gone!" So I stormed my personal flea market before it was declared a national wildlife preserve.

Here's the technique I remember from that book I lost. Pack all the junk you're not using anymore and mark the boxes with today's date two years from now. When that date comes up, chuck out the box without opening it. If you don't miss the stuff in two years, the theory goes, you don't need it anyway. (I suggested that to my wife, and last night while I was sleeping she wrote a date on my forehead.)

Taking Control

Do you ever feel your life is too cluttered? Would you like to simplify it and feel clutter-free? Can you imagine being in control? I'm not only talking about junk that overflows your room and locker and car—I'm also referring to the emotional garbage that buries your soul.

Everyone stores some junk: the grudge against your fifth-grade teacher for humiliating you in class; the anger that still boils toward your ex-boyfriend; the bitterness against an abuser that you refuse to throw away.

Why should you discard the garbage? After all, you were the victim. You're the one with the bruises. Why must *you* forgive? Why must *you* forget?

Perhaps it's because the junk damages you. You're the one who gets buried in it, the one traipsing through life with clutter clanging everywhere. And you're the one who misses the joy of feeling free.

When Jesus told Peter to forgive "not seven times, but seventy-seven times" (Matt. 18:22), He spoke in grace not only for the offender but for the offended as well. As Hannah Moore said: "A Christian will find it cheaper to pardon than to resent. Forgiveness saves the expense of anger, the cost of hatred, the waste of spirits."

The Gospel According to Clutter

Forgiveness is God's way of allowing us to clean up our clutter and live free.

This fabulous news is clearly explained in the Book. (Where did I misplace that Book? I think I saw it last . . .).

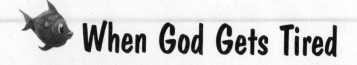

When God Gets Tired

Mr. Pumpernickel was his name. He was short, hairy, and had the breath to kill a moose. But he was the apple of Randy's eye.

Randy purchased Mr. Pumpernickel for $6 from a neighbor. "He's the pick of the litter," the old man boasted. "You'd be hard pressed to find a gerbil with markings like them there. Let alone for $10."

"I got only $6," Randy bargained.

"You got a deal," the old man grinned. "A steal if I do say so myself."

Randy set up Mr. Pumpernickel's home in the corner of the garage. It was a glass castle (10-gallon aquarium) with environmentally friendly carpet. Randy faithfully groomed, fed, exercised, and serenaded him. Without question Mr. Pumpernickel enjoyed a high quality of life—as far as quality goes in a rat's life.

Then came the tragedy. It was a fatal mishap that left Randy stunned and his brother Paul devastated. "I don't know how Mr. Pumpernickel jumped out of the aquarium," Paul explained. "I was just driving the go-cart out of the garage and well, um, somehow he darted in front of me and um, Randy, I am really sorry."

Randy stared in shock at the furry pancake Paul offered him. "You didn't mean to kill him," Randy consented. "That's OK. Let's bury him in the backyard and be done with it."

"Can you ever forgive me?"

"Of course; now let's bury him."

That afternoon the brothers conducted an informal funeral. Randy shoveled a grave while Paul crafted a tombstone made of pine cones.

At 3:00 the next morning Paul couldn't sleep. Visions of Mr. Pumpernickel danced in his head. The guilt tortured him. *How could I kill my brother's favorite pet? his only pet? I'm such a failure. He'll never forgive me. Unless I, um—that's it! Brilliant, Paul! That's it!*

Paul jumped out of bed like a firefighter on duty. Retrieving the shovel in the garage, he raced to the backyard and dug like a prairie dog on speed. Grabbing the stiff gerbil, he hurried to his brother's bed.

"Randy, wake up!" Paul whispered. His brother opened his eyes to see the resurrected rat dangling overhead.

"Uuuuuuuuggggggghhhhhhh! What are you doing?" Randy screamed.

"It's about Mr. Pumpernickel, Randy. Did I ever tell you how sorry I am for what happened?"

"Yes! You moron!"

"I wanted to ask your forgiveness is all," Paul said. "I'm soooooooooooooooo sorry about what happened. I was driving the go-cart too fast, and I didn't see . . ."

"Enough already. It's 3:00 in the morning."

"OK, let's have another funeral; then we'll be done with this thing. I promise."

The boys conducted a beautiful ceremony in honor of the late Mr. Pumpernickel. The episode appeared to be over. Until the next night.

By 3:00 in the morning Paul couldn't toss and turn any longer. That's when another brilliant idea attacked him. *I know! I'll dig up the gerbil and ask Randy's forgiveness. I'll do it now! It's far too important to wait until morning.*

Once again he retrieved the shovel, raced to the backyard, and uncovered the gerbil. He approached his snoring brother.

"Randy, wake up. Did I ever say how sooooooooooooooooo very sorry I am for what I did?"

This story could go on for 50 pages.

And it does—in the lives of many Christians.

How often do we ask God for forgiveness, then insist on digging up past mistakes and dragging them back to Him?

When God assures us that our sins are cast into the ocean, why not leave them buried? When God says "Their sins and lawless acts I will remember no more" (Heb. 10:17), why not believe Him? When God says that Calvary is sufficient, why dig up the dirt of our past? Perhaps even God gets tired of our funerals.

Making the Grade

"Noooooo! Oh, nooooooo! Please don't let it be . . ." I moaned as the door swung open.

"Hello there, Karl!"

Oh, why does he have to visit now? I wondered as Charlie barged into my messy dorm room.

"Is that popcorn I smell?" he asked.

"Yes it is."

"Thought so," he grinned. "I smelled it down the hall. Don't mind if I help myself, do you?"

"Oh no, not at all," I lied.

Why does Charlie always come at the wrong time? I mumbled inside. Of course, there never was a right time for Charlie. But the eve of finals week was definitely wrong.

I gazed at Charlie as he chomped away. His hair was as greasy as the popcorn. His left eye, unable to focus, added a freakishness to his expressions. Skin barely covered his five-foot frame.

Yet despite my cynicism, a tinge of compassion subdued me. Sensing his loneliness, I knew it couldn't be easy for a slightly retarded 31-year-old with the social skills of a cactus to survive on a college campus—even a Christian campus.

"Got any tests tomorrow?" I asked.

"Nope. Don't have no classes this quarter. Mrs. Hinshaw wouldn't let me turn in my back English assignments, so I had to drop her class. She really rips me off. And then I got this ingrown toenail, so I dropped jogging class. Did I show you my ingrown toenail?"

"Yes," I shot back. "You showed it to me last night, remember?"

"Hey! Wanna go get some nachos?"

"I'd love to Charlie, but I got a wicked exam first period tomorrow morning. It's Mr. Russell's class on the Gospel of Matthew."

"Come on! Dad just sent me a check today. It's my treat. We'll get the Monster Plate at El Ponchitos! What do ya say?"

"I can't. I've got an 88.6 percent in the class. If I can just score a 94 or better, I'll pull—"

"I think Tonya wants to go on a date with me," he interrupted as he wiped his greasy hands on my bedspread. "Pretty good popcorn," he added.

Shaking Charlie

Experience taught me that Charlie would pester me the entire evening if I didn't take some kind of action. Hoping to shake him, I got up and roamed down the hall to the water fountain.

But Charlie followed.

Detouring to the lobby to check the mailbox, I persisted in my effort to ditch him.

But Charlie followed.

I stopped for a moment in Dean Lacey's office. Charlie stuck with me like a cocklebur to a spaniel's ear.

"Let's sit here for a bit," he suggested, pointing to the sofa in the lobby. "My toenail's sore. Did I show you my toenail?"

"Great idea!" I beamed.

"OK! I'll get my shoe off and show you!"

"No. I mean, great idea about sitting in the lobby. You rest your toenail, and I'll go study for my test tomorrow."

"You got a test tomorrow?"

"Yeah! A humdinger on the Gospel of Matthew. I'm afraid I'll miss my A if I don't crack down."

"OK, let's go back to your room. I think my toe can make it."

"Don't injure yourself, big guy."

Back in the room, the try-to-shake-Charlie game continued. And Charlie kept winning. He rambled on about the 49ers' season, and Reba McEntire's latest album, and the food in the cafeteria, and on and on and on.

Beep, beep. My watch's hourly alarm beep reminded me that Charlie had wasted 17 minutes of my precious time. The 88.6 percent loomed more and more ominous in my mind.

Charlie blabbered on. "My eye is so bloodshot lately," he continued. "Must be all the videos. Did you see *Disclosure?* I think that was the best . . ."

Then the perfect plan hit me! Why not make a phone call and talk until he leaves? *Brilliant!* I thought. *A splendid strategy, and nobody gets their feelings hurt. It's foolproof!*

"Oh, Charlie!" I interrupted. "I just remembered I need to call Roger." Picking up the phone, I began to dial.

Busy! Oh, Roger! Of all times to be on the phone, why does it have to be now? But hey!—the thought hit me like a bolt of lightning—*how will Charlie ever know the line's busy?*

"Hi, Roger! How ya doing, buddy? Listen, are you ready for Mr. Russell's test tomorrow?"

Breep. Breep. Breep.

"Me neither. I want an A so bad. Do you think he'll ask about the chiastic structure of the Sermon on the Mount?"

Breep. Breep. Breep.

"You want me to come over and help you study?"

Breep. Breep. Breep. The shrill busy signal pierced my ear. Pulling the handset away a bit to preserve my hearing, I forged ahead.

"Yeah, I have got to get a 94 percent! I think I can do it if I don't get sidetracked from studying tonight."

Charlie slouched in the beanbag, fiddling with his scruffy beard. *Will you ever get out of here?* I wondered.

Eight minutes of conversation with a busy signal convinced me the plan wasn't foolproof.

Hanging it up

"Well, Roger, I have got to go study. I'll come over later and study with you. Yeah. OK. Yeah, we'll see ya later. Goodbye."

No sooner had I hung up than Charlie's question pierced like a dagger: "Why did you talk to a busy signal for so long?"

"Um, I, didn't . . ."

"I gotta go," Charlie said.

"Um, well, yeah, OK."

I slumped at my desk. At last, just what I wanted—silence! Oh, how sweet!

After I fumbled through the Bible to Matthew, my gaze focused on Matthew 25:40: "The King will reply, 'I tell you the truth, whatever you did for one of the least of these brothers of mine, you did for me.'"

Silence. Oh, how bittersweet.

Suddenly a 94 percent appeared a little more trivial, while an ingrown toenail seemed a little more important.

Picking up the handset, I dialed once again. But this time I dialed a number that was never busy.

"Hello?"

"Hi, Charlie. Um, I, ah, wanted to, um, ah, you know . . . " Asking forgiveness has never been my spiritual gift. The words caught like sunflower seeds in my throat. "About tonight, I wanted to say, uh, I'm sorry. With the fake phone call and all, um, that was manipulative and scheming. Can you, um, forgive me?"

"Sure. I forgive you. I knew you had to study. I was just waiting to say goodbye."

"Hey, Wednesday my finals are over. Could we go out for the Monster Plate that evening?"

"You bet!"

"Great! And I'll pick up the tab. It's the least I can do."

When Your Feelings Are Crushed

Amber was late for her first class of the school year. Jessica greeted her as she puffed in.

"Wow—look at you," she shouted. "You've added a few pounds over the summer, haven't you? Looks as though you now wear the same size dress as the Statue of Liberty."

The whole class turned and giggled at Amber. She could feel herself turning six shades of red.

"Oh," Jessica gasped, "I didn't mean to embarrass you—forgive me!"

Robert stared at his feet and mumbled to his wife of 13 years. "We never intended for this thing to go this far. It started with us taking our coffee breaks at the same time, and then we began doing lunch together, and, well, one thing led to another."

"But how could you do this to me? to your children?" His wife burned with anger.

"It's nothing against you or the kids. Feelings developed and, um, I'm sorry, it all just got out of hand. Can you ever forgive me?"

Forgiveness is tough work. When the teacher humiliates you for something you didn't do. When your girlfriend betrays you. When your best friend posts your darkest secrets on Internet.

You know the pain. The kind that feels like a jack-hammer to your heart.

Hurt feelings mend slowly. A pain in the neck can heal in a few days, a broken arm within weeks, but hurt feelings can last a lifetime—if we let them.

When our feelings get crushed, we can do several things. We can retaliate with nastier gossip or wallow in our cesspool of misery whining about life's injustice. Perhaps we can attack the offender.

Or we can confront the person in love and confess that our feelings are hurt. Opting for the risky road of truth-telling over peace-keeping, we can surrender our hurt feelings to Jesus.

If anyone understands hurt feelings, it's Jesus. Everyone turned against Him. When He was judged unfairly, not one of His friends came to His defense. Even one of His closest friends cursed Him and denied knowing Him three times.

How did Jesus handle it? Did He fire insults at the traitors? Did He complain on the cross about the injustice of life? Did He slam-dunk Peter with "You slimeball! After all I did for you, you treat Me like this?"

No. He simply forgave them.

We can't protect our feelings from getting hurt. But we can control how we handle the pain.

"A man's wisdom gives him patience; it is to his glory to overlook an offense" (Prov. 19:11).

 # Driving Deals

It was a gargantuan fight over some peewee issue. Since it erupted in the car, the issue was probably driving. More specifically, *my* driving. Now, for the record, there is nothing wrong with my driving. I get 22 miles to the fender. My wife, however, doesn't share my opinion on my ability.

"Would you like to drive?" I asked with the sensitivity of a Brillo pad.

"No. Why?"

"Because you obviously don't like the way I'm driving."

"Did I say that?"

"You don't have to *say* anything. You're as fidgety as a fish on a hook."

"I'm fine. But if you want me to drive, then I'll drive."

"No."

"Why?"

"Because *I'm* driving."

It's not like fighting over the remote control, because if the battle gets ugly there, one person can leave the room. That doesn't work as well if you're doing 60 miles per hour on the freeway.

By the time we arrived home (safely), I was madder than a hornet in a hat. *If she doesn't like my driving,* I reasoned, *then I'll ignore her for the rest of this marriage.* We crawled in bed without even grunting "Good night."

Early the next morning I was reading to my 2-month-old daughter. Coincidentally, I read Matthew 5:23-25— "'Therefore, if you are offering your gift at the altar and there remember that your brother has something against you, leave your gift there in front of the altar. First go and be reconciled to your brother; then come and offer your gift. Settle matters quickly with your adversary'."

I looked into my baby's blue eyes. She can't talk, but boy, can she communicate. She said, "Daddy, are you just going to read this, or do it?"

"Lindsey," I said, "don't talk to your daddy like that."

She kept staring as if to ask "Why not acquiesce your narcissistic amour propre in order to effect a transformation of egotistical wills—thus creating a salubrious environment of reconciled relationships?" Her eyes have an incredible vocabulary.

I said, "Lindsey, if you ever want to see your mother again . . ."

She stared kindly. And God screamed clearly. "Read no further," I sensed His word, "until you ask forgiveness and mend the fractured friendship."

"OK, God, OK," I agreed. "But that doesn't mean she gets to drive today, does it?"

Perspectives on Forgiveness

"When God buries our sins in the deepest sea, He posts a sign that reads No Fishing!"—*Author Unknown.*

"If I say yes I forgive, but I cannot forget as though the God who twice a day washes all the sands on all the shores of all the world could not wash such memories from my mind, then I know nothing of Calvary love. If the living God who made the tide and washes the shores daily cannot wash away from my mind the caustic remarks, the ugliness, the wrongs in someone else, then I haven't even entered into Calvary love."—Amy Carmichael.

"Forgiveness is the fragrance the violet sheds on the heel that has crushed it."—*Author Unknown.*

"For if you forgive men when they sin against you, your heavenly Father will also forgive you. But if you do not forgive men their sins, your Father will not forgive your sins."—Matthew 6:14, 15.

"It took me a long time to learn that God is not the enemy of His enemies."—Martin Niemoller.

"Everyone says forgiveness is a lovely idea, until they have something to forgive."—C. S. Lewis.

"Don't carry a grudge. While you're carrying the grudge the other guy's out dancing."—Buddy Hackett.

"He who cannot forgive others breaks the bridge over which he must pass himself."—George Herbert.

"Always forgive your enemies—nothing annoys them so much."—Oscar Wilde.

"'Come now, let us reason together,'" says the Lord. "'Though your sins are like scarlet, they shall be as white as snow; though they are red as crimson, they shall be like wool.'"—Isaiah 1:18.

The Gospel
According to Ketchup

Hopeless End?
Or Endless Hope?

I get as rankled as the next guy over life's irritations: canker sores, cigarette smoke, cheek-pinching relatives, junk mail that looks as though it contains a real check, cold toilet seats, etc. But nothing—and I mean nothing—annoys me quite the way Heinz ketchup does.

I'm towering over a mountain of french fries at Denny's. The greasy steam tickles my nostrils. I sprinkle the salt. And grab my fork. My stomach is pumped for action. My taste buds vibrate with anticipation.

Then the attendant delivers the Heinz ketchup. I pop the cap and tip the bottle. And wait.

And wait.

And wait.

And wait.

Shouldn't that be against the law? Who gave Heinz the right to make us sing 36 verses of "anticipaaaaay-aaay-aay-tion" before we chow down? Doesn't seem fair.

But it always seems worth it. When the sauce finally

drips, the reward is far greater than the delay.

So I keep ordering and waiting. And after waiting long enough, my hope always receives its reward. The gospel according to Heinz ketchup rings true: tasty things come to those who wait.

So what are you waiting for? What's in your portfolio of hope? Perhaps your hopes intersect with these: my parents will reconcile; my biology teacher will let the B+ slide as an A-; I'll make a six-digit salary; I'll see my aborted baby in heaven someday; I'll get my driver's license; Jesus will come soon.

Whatever your hopes, keep hoping. Ignore the cynics such as Woody Allen, who said, "More than any other time in history, mankind faces a crossroads. One path leads to despair and utter hopelessness; the other to total extinction. Let us pray we have the wisdom to choose correctly."

Be advised: cynics aren't always right. Consider instead the words of Gilbert Beenken: "Other men see only a hopeless end, but the Christian rejoices in an endless hope."

So keep hoping. And savor the delicacy of ketchup-covered fries.

**"Be strong and take heart,
all you who hope in the Lord"
(Ps. 31:24).**

Pummeled by Blue Jays

Our expectations soared as we shuffled into the Kingdome. The Seattle Mariners were hosting the Toronto Blue Jays. My wife and I bought soft pretzels, drinks, peanuts, popcorn, and Cracker Jack, and settled into our seats in center field. We were set to watch a great game.

At the top of the first inning, however, the Mariners' pitcher walked a batter. He tattooed the next guy with a wild pitch. The next Blue Jay loaded the bases with a finesse bunt down the first-base line. That sent John Olerud to the plate. With one swing, Olerud blasted a souvenir straight to the fan sitting a few rows below us.

Unable to do anything in the bottom of the first, the Mariners quickly returned to the outfield. That's when things went from ugly to hideous. By the end of the second inning the score was 11 to zip.

The players knew it, and we knew it—the game was over. But we hadn't even opened our boxes of Cracker Jack!

A chubby guy wearing a red flannel shirt and a teal hat arrived late and sat beside us. Not believing the scoreboard, he asked, "That ain't really the score, is it?"

I assured him it was. "Holy macaroni!" he fumed. "There ain't no use watching this one." He left as quickly as he had come.

The disgruntled fan was right. The Mariners were *not* going to come back from 11 to nothing.

The players looked discouraged. Angry fans were booing and throwing things. Even the mascot, the Mariner Moose (who can usually outlast the Energizer Bunny), lost all enthusiasm. What a disaster!

My wife wanted to join the hordes of fans clogging the exits. Being a fourth-generation Seventh-day Adventist, however, I was too cheap to leave. So we stayed until the brutal end.

My wife slept while I entertained myself with irrational thoughts. *Wouldn't it be great,* I mused, *if I could reset the score to 0-0—right now in the third inning? With that score, our players' hope would be revived and they'd start playing with intensity. The fans would start hoping for a hometown victory again. My wife would wake up—and we could finish all this junk food!*

Resetting a blowout score in the third inning is how forgiveness works. Forgiveness breathes optimism into desperate situations. It revives the hopeless. And cleans the slate.

Perhaps you feel overwhelmed by past mistakes. That's when the gospel intervenes with an irrational miracle. When the scoreboard shows that Satan is winning, Jesus declares the new score is 0-0 again. Our sins are forgiven. Our errors are erased. It's a whole new ball game. Once again we have hope!

**"Therefore, my brothers,
I want you to know that through Jesus
the forgiveness of sins is proclaimed
to you" (Acts 13:38).**

 # Deadly State

Light through the stained glass spills rust and red and orange on my grandpa's bald head. The colors reflect off his glasses. As the organ moans "When Peace Like a River," the preacher organizes his notes. Our family sits in the front pew, consumed with memories of Grandpa.

Karl, we do not want you to be ignorant about your grandpa, who has fallen asleep, or to grieve like the rest of men, who have no hope.*

They are good memories. I remember sitting on his lap in the 1964 Ford Galaxie 500XL and giggling as "the magic seat" would automatically glide forward at the push of a button. I remember the explosion of laughter when Grandpa triumphantly slammed down "the birdie" in a Rook game. I remember the A & W root beer floats. And darebase. And groaning out one more pull-up at his encouraging.

We believe that Jesus died and rose again and so we believe that God will bring with Jesus your grandpa who has fallen asleep in Him.

Grandpa planted a big garden, broke up fights, pulled the grandkids in his wagon, grumbled about church politics, chuckled at Archie Bunker, sported soiled overalls, and sparkled when the topic of conversation drifted to rock hunting. He didn't do anything unusual—only did what lots of grandpas do: smother his grandkids with love.

I'd Rather Kiss a Catfish

According to the Lord's own word, we tell you that we who are still alive, who are left till the coming of the Lord, will certainly not precede your grandpa, who has fallen asleep.

He comes to mind when I smell Old Spice cologne and when I taste a real sour pickle. When a hearing aid squeals in somebody's ear, I can still hear him grumbling, "These lousy things!" And, of course, I can't attend a funeral without reminiscing.

For the Lord Himself will come down from heaven, with a loud command, with the voice of the archangel and with the trumpet call of God, and your grandpa will rise first.

Grandpa's fire has gone out. The winds of age extinguished his struggling flame. Although the embers that remain burn only in our memories, we who believe hold strong to God's promise that Grandpa's fire will flame anew.

After that, we who are still alive and are left will be caught up together with your grandpa in the clouds to meet the Lord in the air. And so we will be with the Lord forever. Therefore encourage each other with these words.

The Day Jesus Came

Three o'clock in the morning. The phone rings, awakening my father just enough for him to grumble, "Hello?"

"Isn't it wonderful, Pastor?" the aged voice says excitedly.

"Huh? What are you talking about?" My dad wonders if he's dreaming.

"Have you looked outside, Pastor?"

"What are you talking about?" My dad peers outside into the darkness.

"It's dark! It's dark, Pastor. This is it!"

"Yeah? So?"

"No more arthritis! No more glaucoma! No more wheelchair! Soon I'll be in my new heavenly body. Jesus is here at last!"

By now my father understands. "Mrs. Charles," he says gently, "do you know it's 3:00 in the *morning?*"

"Huh? No, Pastor, it's 3:00 in the afternoon and look how dark it is! Jesus is coming. All things are made new."

"No, Mrs. Charles. It's nighttime. That's why it's dark outside."

"Are you sure, Pastor?"

"Yes, Mrs. Charles."

"Oh, Pastor, I'm terribly sorry. I thought it was the afternoon and . . . I mean, I just assumed Jesus was . . . what I'm saying is . . . I feel so silly. I'm sorry. It must be this new medication Dr. Darcy put me on. Oh, Pastor, you go back to bed. I'm sorry. Good night."

I wish I could say Jesus came that night and took Mrs. Charles into the clouds of glory. I wish that that evening God had destroyed her wheelchair and smoothed her wrinkles and restored the bounce in her step as she sailed toward heaven.

But Mrs. Charles is dead now. Her home has been replaced with an Exxon Minimart.

Last summer, when I visited the old New England church where I knew Mrs. Charles, many pews were empty. The years have eroded the storybook church of my memories. I wish I could report of a vibrant church . . . but I can't.

I wish I could make that church new again. I wish I could return to kindergarten and sing "Happy, Happy Home," and grimace at the slobbery greetings of the old ladies, and fidget in the pew during my dad's sermon. I wish I could restore the vigor and enthusiasm as I remember it . . . but I can't.

I wish I could rebuild the neighborhood I grew up in. I'd replace the gangs with the carefree kids I remember. I'd exchange the drug dealers that now rule Johnston Creek Park with the Little Leaguers of my childhood. If I could make all things new, I would . . . but I can't.

But God can.

So I tenaciously hold to His promise: "Now we look forward with confidence to our heavenly bodies, realizing that every moment we spend in these earthly bodies is time spent away from our eternal home in heaven with Jesus" (2 Cor. 5:6, TLB).

A Kodak Moment With Lorrie Morgan

I have all her albums and can sing you any song she has recorded. (Warning: when I sing I sound like a hippo in heat!) Even have a couple compact discs a friend of a friend asked her to autograph for me as a Christmas present: "To Karl, Best Wishes, Lorrie Morgan." When it comes to music, give me Nashville. And when it comes to country music, give me Lorrie Morgan.

For five years now I have waited for Lorrie's tour to hit Seattle. Last night she came! Seven-member band. Enough lights to illuminate Rhode Island. And a show that sparked the audience to four standing ovations.

Quite a concert it was. But her encore overshadowed it. Not her dazzling *Something in Red* number. Or her *War Paint* encore. I mean her encore encore. Her after-almost-everybody-left encore.

While we shuffled out of the Opera House, someone rumored, "If you want to meet Lorrie Morgan, stick around."

"Really?" My buddy Arlyn and I froze. "Suppose we could?"

"Who knows?" I said. "Let's see."

So we plopped in the cushy seats and waited. And waited. And waited.

About 50 people stayed—all of us banking on a long shot. Riding a rumor. Hoping to meet Lorrie.

"I don't think she's coming out," I moaned 30 minutes later. "Let's go."

"Hold on," Arlyn insisted. "Be patient. She'll come."

The man in the white cowboy hat gave up. As did the woman with a Lorrie Morgan T-shirt. Slowly the number of waiting fans dwindled to a faithful few.

But we waited.

While we were waiting, my mind drifted to a chapter on hope. I thought of another small group of faithful followers waiting to meet Someone. Some call us crazy. "You're banking on a long shot." "You're riding a rumor." "Keep dreaming—Jesus will never come back."

But we wait. And hope. Because the Bible is clear: be patient. Remain faithful. Don't give up. Jesus *is* coming!

And when He comes, our judgment will be sealed. His words will echo through the universe: "Let him who does wrong continue to do wrong; . . . let him who does right continue to do right" (Rev. 22:11). Enough is enough, and that's that.

To all who place their hope in Jesus, the day of judgment is good news! For it is a showcase of His grace and mercy to sinners.

The Judgment

The old man had been caught stealing a loaf of bread. As he trembled before Judge La Guardia in New York he explained that he had taken the bread because his family was starving.

"Well, I have to punish you," Judge La Guardia said. "The law makes no exception, and I have no choice but to fine you $10."

The man swallowed hard. His eyes moistened. Where could he ever get $10 when he didn't even have enough money for bread in the first place? The judge's sentence was beyond his ability to pay.

But then the judge did the strangest thing. "The law is the law," he said as he pulled out his wallet, "but here's

The Gospel According to Ketchup

the $10 to pay your fine.

"Furthermore," he said, tossing another dollar into his hat, "I am going to fine everyone in the courtroom 50 cents for living in a town in which a man has to steal bread in order to eat." So he passed the hat, and the old man left the courtroom with $47.50.

The best word to describe the judge's action is *grace.* Grace is getting the opposite of what you deserve. It's the word that best describes God's action toward us. According to God's law, the penalty of sin is death. On the day of judgment we deserve to die. Like the old man, we are guilty, with no hope of paying for our wrongdoing.

The law is the law, and the penalty must be paid. That's when God did the strangest thing. He paid the penalty Himself. Then He gave us the wonderful free gift of eternal life.

All we have to do is accept it. And wait until He returns to receive it.

So be patient. Remain faithful. Guard your hope. Jesus *is* coming with your gift! And it will be worth the wait!

By the way, my wait for Lorrie was worthwhile as well. I got a picture with her arm around me to prove it!

 # Perspectives on Hope

"Cynicism is cancer of the spirit. The bad cells of sarcasm attack the good cells of hope and, if undiagnosed, will eventually destroy them."—Fred Smith.

"Now, a crown is waiting for me. I will get that crown for being right with God. The Lord is the judge who judges rightly, and he will give me the crown on that Day. He will give that crown not only to me but to all those who have waited with love for him to come again."—2 Timothy 4:8, EB.

"For the Christian, the dark shadow of death will be illuminated by the shining face of Jesus."—*Author Unknown.*

"To be a sinner is our distress, but to know it is our hope." Fulton Sheen

A California woman wrote, "No matter how bad the pain is, it's never so bad that suicide is the only answer. Suicide doesn't end pain. It only lays it on the broken shoulders of the survivors." And she ends her story. "By the way: to all the doctors, nurses, and psychiatrists who forced me to live when I didn't want to—thank you for keeping breath in my lungs and my heart beating and encouraging hope in me when I didn't have any hope."—*Newsweek,* Feb. 7, 1983.

"Jesus planted the only durable rumor of hope amid the widespread despair of a hopeless world."—Carl F. Henry.

"So this body that ruins will clothe itself with that which never ruins. And this body that dies will clothe itself with that which never dies. When this happens, then this Scripture will be made true: 'Death is destroyed forever in victory. Death, where is your victory? Death, where is your power to hurt?'"—1 Corinthians 15:54, 55, EB.

"Without Christian culture and Christian hope, the modern world would come to resemble a half-derelict fun-fair, gone nasty and poverty-racked, one enormous Atlantic City."—Russell Kirk.

"Everything that is done in the world is done by hope."—Martin Luther.

The Gospel
According to Giggles

Chill Out and Have Fun!

"And he said: 'I tell you the truth, unless you change and become like little children, you will never enter the kingdom of heaven'" (Matt. 18:3).

What did Jesus mean when He said we'd better become like kids or we'll never see the pearly gates?

Did He mean we must develop a childlike trust? That's part of it. Was He saying we should be innocent like kids? Sure. Perhaps He was calling us to demonstrate a child's humility.

Or maybe He was also saying we ought to chill out and have more fun—like kids. Bingo! That's my read on it.

Sorry, Brother Boring, but Jesus had a child's heart. Not just a heart for children, but a child's heart. A heart bursting with song and exploding with creativity and joy. A heart drawn to parties and weddings and children. A heart that had a passion to play.

Maybe these thoughts surprise you. After all, it's not everybody who pegs Jesus as a party animal. But He had that side to Him. His foes accused Him of eating too much, drinking too much, and hanging out with the riffraff (Matt. 11:19). I'm sad to report that it's been a long time since someone accused me of having too much fun. How about you?

Why is it that play comes so easy to children, but as we grow older, rigor mortis of the funny bone sets in?

Why not let someone else worry about running the world today? Jesus took time to play with kids; why don't we?

So bring out the Tootsie Rolls (so what if it sticks to your teeth?).

Bring out the Pictionary (so what if your stick figures look like funky lizards?).

Giggle. Loosen up. Dip your Oreos in milk until they get really soggy. Take a nap. Build a sand castle. Gargle some root beer. Squish mud through your toes. Hitchhike through a car wash. Try yodeling. Be a child today.

Or, if you prefer the biblical word, celebrate!

101 Things
I'm Thankful For

Q-tips after a hot shower ☺ waterfalls ☺ broccoli and mushrooms—my two favorite foods ☺ Ben and Jerry's Chunky Monkey Ice Cream ☺ eagles (and birdies and pars) ☺ my dad (who still treats Mom as if she were the first lady) ☺ my mom (who still bakes my favorite mint chocolate-chip birthday cake) ☺ Jesus ☺ Caesar salads ☺ my algebra teacher ☺ a 4-year-old's imagination ☺ Romans 8:28 ☺ warranties ☺ Easter ☺ *National Geographic* ☺ Bob and Donna and Warren (church leaders who do things with style and class) ☺ computers ☺ the stranger on Interstate 5 who stopped when I ran out of gas ☺ Plentywood, Montana ☺ sandboxes ☺ camping in the Nimrod ☺ Grandpa ☺ sunsets ☺ country music ☺ Milton and DeDe's getaway cabin on Whidbey Island ☺ my wife (who still laughs at my stale jokes) ☺ Rook ☺ Sammy (an adorable Labrador retriever) ☺ assurance of salvation ☺ a church family that walks on water ☺ strong health ☺ forgiveness ☺ my Corolla (ready to celebrate its "quarter-of-a-million-miles" birthday) ☺ gut laughs ☺ stories with surprise endings ☺ great musical groups of the seventies) ☺ the story of Joseph ☺ lightning bugs ☺ strolls on brick-paved roads lined with eighteenth-century houses ☺ cranberry sauce ☺ off-the-cuff compliments ☺ thunderstorms ☺ bubble gum ☺ eagles ☺ halvah ☺ crayons ☺ Psalm 23 ☺ bobolinks ☺ rainbow-colored fires ☺ Calvary ☺ Swiss cheese ☺ cream puffs ☺ *America's Funniest Home Videos* ☺ precariously tall lemon meringue ☺ John 3:16 ☺ circular couches ☺ David Letterman ☺ snowballs ☺ errant clouds chasing each other across the sky ☺ drive-in root beer mugs ☺ "O Holy Night" ☺

barbershop quartets ☺ 1 Corinthians 13 ☺ soft pretzels with grains of course salt, served with sunny yellow mustard ☺ my daughter Lindsey ☺ discovering there's a second layer of chocolates ☺ class reunions ☺ impromptu vespers on Friday evenings ☺ Christmas trees draped with strings of popcorn and candy canes ☺ porch swings ☺ Monopoly's most-landed-on properties: Illinois Avenue, B&O Railroad, free parking, Tennessee Avenue, New York Avenue, Reading Railroad, St. James Place, Waterworks, and Pennsylvania Railroad ☺ happy auroras ☺ 6:00 a.m. newspaper deliveries ☺ bamboo bird cages ☺ ventriloquism ☺ the promise of Jesus' Second Coming ☺ modular storage systems ☺ fish tank bubbles ☺ Warren Dunes State Park, Michigan ☺ a sense of humor early in the morning ☺ Costco ☺ *The Far Side* ☺ red, white, and blue ☺ 1961 ☺ a ripe pear ☺ Log Cabin syrup tins ☺ the bicycle path around Green Lake ☺ Table Mountain in Cape Town, South Africa ☺ soft, wet kisses and big, hardy hugs ☺ a carpet of wild strawberries ☺ the Sermon on the Mount ☺ spontaneity ☺ Sunday mornings with cartoons, pajamas, and a big bowl of Captain Crunch ☺ the 10 most beautiful words: chimes, dawn, golden, hush, lullaby, luminous, melody, mist, murmuring, tranquil ☺ homemade muffins ☺ April Fools' Day ☺ behind-the-scenes editors ☺ rainbows ☺ the empty stretches of bun on either end of a hot dog ☺ drivers who yield to other drivers ☺ the Bible.

Your Turn

You know what? I feel 101 times better after writing this list! Focusing on what you're thankful for is therapeutic. So get a slip of paper and write your own chapter. You'll be glad you did!

"Give thanks to the Lord, for he is good" (Ps. 136:1).

 Laughter After all

I laugh whenever I think of her, though I've never met her or talked to her. But her anger has brought me a gallon of joy. Hers was an anonymous voice inquiring about an anger management seminar.

"Sorry, but our church doesn't offer an anger management seminar," my assistant kindly informed her.

"But I saw it advertised on the reader board at your church," the woman insisted.

"I don't know of anything like that. Perhaps you're thinking of our Lost Relationship Support Group or our Addicts Anonymous."

"Then why are you advertising it on your sign?" the woman snipped.

"I've worked here for more than a year and am in charge of the messages on the reader board, and I know we've never advertised an anger management seminar since I've been here."

"This is North Creek Christian Fellowship of Seventh-day Adventists, isn't it?" Her pitch jumped an octave per sentence.

"Yes ma'am, but we don't . . . "

"There ought to be a law against you *##*#^*#@! Christians who use false advertising to sucker people into your cult."

"I'm afraid you're mistaking us for some other . . . "

"Why *don't* you offer an anger management class?" the woman demanded. "There is a big need, you know."

"Yes, I can see that!" The woman's anger over no anger management class struck my assistant as being funny. She tried to swallow her giggles.

"Noooooo! Dimwit!" the woman exploded. "The class isn't for me! It's for my husband!"

Fortunately the woman slammed the phone down before my assistant burst into laughter.

I still laugh when I think of her. Forgive me if that seems insensitive. I don't laugh at her problem with anger—I share her problem. Rather, I laugh at the irony in life. And I whisper a prayer of thanks for the moments of irony that pepper our lives with humor.

Why do some people choose to make life a grim marathon of frowns? Must we sacrifice our sense of humor on the altar of adulthood? Must the world be a mortuary? Must we allow grouches to squelch the music of life?

Forgive me, Deacon Dirge and Sister Sourpuss, but I believe Christians ought to be more than a gloomy bunch of pious poops with the personality of soggy Cream of Wheat. It's time to shatter the long faces some Christians are known for.

We're called to reflect the joy of Jesus. Liking parties better than theological debates, He carved out time for kids and feasts. He enjoyed funny stories that slam-dunked religious know-it-alls. I think Jesus laughed when the pious woman got ticked off because we couldn't cure her "husband's" anger problem.

You see, the Jesus I know opts for laughter after all. Won't it be fun to be with Jesus and enjoy laughter ever after?

**"My heart leaps for joy
and I will give thanks to him in song"
(Ps. 28:7).**

The Chuckle File

Laughter is a sacred sound to God. Splashing color, richness, and texture onto the drab canvas of life, it is a gift, a choice, a discipline, and an art. It is a massage for the soul.

So if you don't mind, I'm going to dig up my humor folder and share some stories that have amused me.

If you don't feel like laughing with me, close the book or turn the page. Far be it from me to make you smile.

※ ※ ※

Grandma and her granddaughter, an energetic 10-year-old, were spending an evening together when the girl asked, "How old are you, Grandma?"

"Well, sweetie, when you're as old as I am, you don't share your age with anybody."

"Aw, come on, Grandma, you can trust me."

"Oh no, my sweet one, I won't tell anybody my age."

Grandma got busy fixing supper and then realized her sweetie had been absent for 20 minutes—much too long! She searched the house and discovered her granddaughter had dumped the contents of her purse all over the bedroom floor. The granddaughter sat in the middle of the mess, triumphantly raising her grandma's driver's license.

When Grandma entered the room the child announced: "Grandma, you're 76."

"That's right. How did you know that?"

"I found the date of your birthday here on your driver's license and subtracted that year from this year . . . so you're 76."

"Very good. You're right, I am 76."

The little girl continued staring at the driver's license and added, "You also made an F in sex."

₩ ₩ ₩

A man comes out of a shopping mall to find that the side of his parked car had been rammed in. Seeing a note under the windshield wiper, he reads it: "As I'm writing this, about a dozen people are watching me. They think I'm giving you my name, phone number, and insurance company. But I'm not."

₩ ₩ ₩

My file is stuffed with hundreds more, but that's enough for now. I feel better already, don't you?

Oh, before I go I want to share one more story, one that I heard just tonight.

I was chatting with the umpire before my city-league softball game. He talked of his first day as a sixth grader in a new school.

"Since we had just moved to Wenatchee, everything seemed strange," he said. "I felt lost in the new surroundings. Everyone seemed so hostile, especially the teacher.

"Before class began, I raised my hand and said, 'Mrs. Campbell, I didn't sign up for advanced math. I'm supposed to be in the other session.'

"Her rude response floored me. 'Go to hell and wait,' she snapped.

"I burst out the door in tears. Racing to the pay phone in the lobby, I called home. 'Dad,' I sobbed, 'I hate this new school! Everyone's mean. Even the teacher cussed at me . . . yes she did . . . did too . . . they put me in the wrong class and when I told her so she barked that I should go to hell and wait . . . I ain't staying in this stupid school . . .'

"Just then a kindly old woman interrupted my phone conversation. 'Young man,' she said, 'I couldn't help overhearing you. I think you misunderstood. She sent you to me. I'm the registrar—Helen Waite.'"

"A cheerful heart is good medicine" (Prov. 17:22).

 Surprise!

"Surprise!" I think it's my favorite word (well, OK, next to "a la mode"). Surprises are the bubbles in life's wellspring of joy. Whether it's a letter of affirmation, an unexpected phone call, or the hug of reassurance, surprises drain the monotony out of life.

I love giving surprises. You know that if you read the dedication page of my first book:

"Dedicated to my wife, Cherié.

"Whether it's scrunching into a birthday present . . .

We were to be separated for a year. Cherié thought I was in Africa. Instead, I flew across the country to hide in a birthday present with my camera poised. When she ripped into the present, she was some kind of surprised. I've got a picture of her esophagus to prove it!

"or snapping pictures of a Hershey bomb . . .

I proposed in a sewer field. That may not sound romantic, but hear me out. While we were photographing a spectacular sunset, a plane buzzed us overhead. Suddenly a box dropped from it. Fearing it was a bomb, Cherié refused to open it. Finally she did, and discovered a thousand Hershey Kisses cushioning a proposal.

"or an escort to the deck of Festivale . . .

Our honeymoon was a surprise. Cherié hadn't a clue where we were going until we flew to Miami and our taxi driver delivered us to a cruise ship.

"you punctuate life with surprise.

On birthdays and Groundhog Day, ordinary days and special days, Cherié has orchestrated some doozy surprises of her own.

". . . Here's one more.

"HAPPY BIRTHDAY!"

Cherié had no clue I was working on a book; that is, until she opened her birthday present last year and read the dedication page.

Some surprises refresh us. Other surprises rebuke us.

Such as the young man whose story was featured in a recent Dear Abby column. He was from a wealthy family, about to graduate from high school. It was a custom in his affluent community for parents to give their graduating children a new car, and the boy and his dad had spent weeks visiting one dealership after another. The week before graduation they found the perfect car. The boy was certain it would be in the driveway on graduation night.

On the eve of his graduation, however, his father handed him a small package wrapped in colorful paper. It was a Bible! The boy was so angry he threw the Bible down and stormed out of the house. He and his father never saw each other again.

Several years later the news of the father's death finally brought the son home again. Following the funeral, he sat alone one evening, going through his father's possessions that he was to inherit, when he came across the Bible his dad had given him. Overwhelmed by grief, he brushed away the dust and cracked it open for the first time. When he did, a cashier's check dated the day of his high school graduation fell into his lap—in the exact amount of the car they had chosen together. Rebuked by surprise!

Whether we're refreshed or rebuked by them, let's remember that surprises are God's way of reminding us that He is still in charge. As we navigate through the surprising potholes of life, let's keep in mind that God does all things well. He can be trusted. Surprisingly, such is the secret of joy.

"Trust in the Lord with all your heart and lean not on your own understanding; in all your ways acknowledge him, and he will make your paths straight" (Prov. 3:5, 6).

 # Perspectives on Joy

"Be happy while you're living, for you're a long time dead."—Scottish proverb.

"The cheerful heart has a continual feast."—Proverbs 15:15.

"Happiness is the practice of virtues."—Clement of Alexandria.

No language has as many words for joy and rejoicing as does Hebrew. In the Old Testament 13 Hebrew roots, found in 27 different words, are used primarily for some aspect of joy or joyful participation in religious worship. Hebrew religious ritual demonstrates God as the source of joy.

"Joy is never in our power, and pleasure is. I doubt whether anyone who has tasted joy would ever, if both were in his power, exchange it for all the pleasure in the world."—C. S. Lewis.

"We are all strings in the concert of his joy."—Jakob Boehme.

"If you obey my commands, you will remain in my love, just as I have obeyed my Father's commands and remain in his love. I have told you this so that my joy may be in you and that your joy may be complete"—John 15:10, 11.

"Happiness is parking on what's left of the last guy's quarter."—Milton Berle.

"Laughter can turn a 36-hour day back into a 24-hour day."—Bumper sticker.

"Ask yourself whether you are happy, and you cease to be so."—John Stuart Mill.

"The fountain of delight bubbling with true joy and laughter is still to be found in the worship of our Lord and Saviour Jesus Christ."—Dan Martella.

"Some people think it's difficult to be a Christian and to laugh, but I think it's the other way around. God writes a lot of comedy; it's just that He has so many bad actors."—Garrison Keillor.

"Should we not see that lines of laughter about the eyes are just as much marks of faith as are the lines of care and seriousness? Is it only earnestness that is baptized? Is laughter pagan? We have already allowed too much that is good to be lost to the church and cast many pearls before swine. A church is in a bad way when it banishes laughter from the sanctuary and leaves it to the cabaret, the night-club, and the toastmasters."—Helmut Thielicke.

"Finally, my brothers, rejoice in the Lord!"—Philippians 3:1.

The Gospel
According to Platypuses

Funny Beaks and Big Tails

To look at the platypus, you'd think that after creation God threw together a bunch of leftover parts. "Watch this, angels," maybe God smiled, "I'll slap a duck bill on one end and a beaver tail on the other!"

It's hard to tell what a platypus is. Although it's a mammal, it lays eggs. It has webbed feet but walks on its knuckles. And it has eyes but no external ears. Talk about an identity crisis!

One would be hard-pressed to stare a platypus in the beak and argue that God has no sense of humor. Even the name carves a grin on my face. How would you like to be called "platypus"? "Hi, I'm your doctor, Platypus Smith . . ."

With all these strikes against it, however, I have yet to see a platypus try to be another animal. I couldn't blame it for doing so. Wouldn't you rather be an eagle or a jaguar or a racehorse? I would. But not the platypus. It blunders along, content to be the peculiar klutz with a duck's beak and a beaver's tail—just as God created it. Which is precisely what makes the platypus so cool.

Have you ever wondered if God goofed when He created you? Perhaps you don't like your funny beak or your big tail. So you try to be somebody you're not, and in the process you flop like a platypus trying to soar as an eagle. It's frustrating and phony to be anybody but yourself. Instead, you should rejoice in your individuality.

The gospel according to platypuses reminds us that each of us is a unique creation of God—freckles, flat feet, big nose, crooked dimples, funny ribs, and everything else. You were created like nobody else, and *you* matter to God. He designed you especially as He wanted *you*. And He died on a cross because He especially wanted *you*.

So if God created you like a platypus, relax! Get comfortable with your own style, looks, and hang-ups. That's precisely what makes you so cool.

"Each one should test his own actions.
Then he can take pride in himself, without
comparing himself to somebody else"
(Gal. 6:4).

Special Delivery

Everybody has a baby. I'm telling you, baby-having is a wildly popular thing. Bigger than the hula hoop.

For my wife and me, it wasn't enough that *all* our friends had babies. They expected *us* to have one too.

"When are you going to have a baby?" they persisted. "You really *must* have a baby."

"Why?"

"Well, because. You don't know about sleepless nights without a baby."

"So?"

"And without a baby, you can enjoy an uninterrupted, grown-up conversation."

"Yeah?"

"And the tax advantages."

"Now you're talking cents."

"And besides, you'll never understand God's love for us until you experience it with your own child."

"OK. OK. Where do we sign up?" The spiritual stab always cuts deepest. Of course we wanted to understand God's love for us. But first we wanted to get our relationship, our careers, our finances, the federal deficit, and the universe in order before we jumped into anything crazy.

Finally we grew weary of being the only baby-free couple on earth who remembers Kennedy's assassination, so we decided to join the parenting ranks. The problem is—and don't miss this subtle point of parenting—child rearing doesn't start with your kid graduating from medical school. If more parents understood this, they'd probably stop having babies, and the medical community would have to go into the used-computer business. But ignorance reigns and the business is still booming, so I'll give you my read on this baby-having venture.

BC—Before Child

Before you can meet your baby, you have to attend childbirth classes in which you openly talk about internal organs with strangers. Our instructor focused on the uterus, since that's where babies hang out before birth. As I recall, the ovum starts growing there and rapidly divides into zillions of specialized parts—not unlike the federal government. Within seven weeks it has developed all the tools it needs to drool. By 10 weeks it has the ability to cry in church.

When we weren't discussing the uterus, we were learning how to breathe. Breathing is important, because if you don't do it in the delivery room, your odds of success get dramatically reduced. Really. So we spent lots of time on the floor with pillows. The women faked contractions while the men pretended to time them. After several weeks of practicing this deep breathing, my wife and I believed our delivery would be painless. Obviously we were hyperventilating.

All in all, the childbirth classes were most enlightening. How else would I have learned that gynecologists use chrome-plated instruments that resemble industrial can openers? Armed with weeks of wisdom, we entered the delivery room—without a clue.

Happy Birthday!

"Happy birthday" is an oxymoron. The only happy person on our daughter's birthday was the accountant. The rest of us felt like we were skinny-dipping in a pool of hot tar.

"You're doing great, Cherié! Just great!" I coaxed. "Isn't she?"

"Oh, um, ah, yeah! Real great!" The doctor and nurse agreed.

"Arrrruuuuuuggggggghhhhhhhh!" Cherié seemed unusually cranky. So I cracked a very funny joke. Normally she laughs at my very funny jokes. This time she didn't laugh. Instead she squeezed the pulse out of my wrist.

Whenever the contractions eased, I broached the volatile topic of naming our miracle. It was a challenge. Since we were the last parents of the Woodstock era to give birth, our friends had already taken all of our first choices. Charity, Faith, Serenity, Visualize, Granola, World—all classic names, but taken. "How about something unusual, like Bob?" I suggested.

"I hate Bob. My first boyfriend's dog was named Bob. Besides, the baby is a girl."

Since I was making no progress on name selection, I stuck with coaching. "Breathe, two, three, four. Breathe . . . "

The doctor and nurse were coaching from the other end of the bed. We sounded like a group of genuinely sincere people trying to help a grizzly dislodge a Cadillac from its throat.

"You're doing great, Cherié! Just great," I coaxed. "Isn't she?"

We repeated this cycle for 20 hours until our kid came out and immediately demanded to be put back in. One look at that beautiful child, however, and I wouldn't have returned her for all the sleep-filled nights and adult conversations in the world. Never have I so desperately wanted to join the sleepless in Seattle.

AD—After Delivery

Now, we had been duly warned that newborns resemble Mr. Potato Head covered in slime. But not Lindsey.

She was prettier than a tax refund. This child looked nothing like the ugly babies you see in the sex education movies. She was God's most perfect creation to date.

I pictured God smiling with me at His cherished work of art. "Knitted together" is how the psalmist described this miracle of God creating Lindsey. Each thread of character carefully selected. Every fiber of temperament deliberately intertwined.

God as her Creator.

A poet, searching for the precise word.

An artist, blending the exact color.

A musician, creating an exquisite masterpiece.

The Creator. Weaving together a soul like no other: Lindsey Kay Haffner.

"For you created my inmost being; you knit me together in my mother's womb" (Ps. 139:13).

What are you Worth?

How do you determine your value?
Some find their value in *performance* . . .
"I can dunk a basketball."
"I am a 4.0 student."
"I play the piano like Dino."
Some find their value in *possessions* . . .
"I drive a hot Corvette."
"My wardrobe is exclusively Ralph Lauren."
"I've got the top-of-the-line snowboard."
Still others find their value in *position* . . .
"I was accepted to Harvard."
"I am the youngest senior vice-president in the history of the company."
"I am Student Association president."

So what's the right answer? What is your value? To answer, consider how value is determined.

Recently Barbra Streisand sold a few of her valuables. She explained, "I want only two houses, rather than seven . . . I feel like letting go of things." (Tsk, tsk, poor darling—how will she survive with only *two* homes?) So she sent her Tiffany cobweb lamp to the auction—and it fetched a cool $717,500. What, pray tell, makes that lamp any more valuable than the K Mart special that sits on my desk? My lamp shines as bright as hers. Why is mine worth $6 and hers worth a corner of Fort Knox?

What determines value?

Value is determined by what somebody is willing to pay for it. At the same auction Streisand sold a nude painting of Adam and Eve for nearly $2 million. What makes the painting so valuable? That's what somebody coughed up for it.

What a Hoot!

Recently some neighbors held a garage sale. The following day I asked how it went.

"It was incredible!" my neighbor beamed. "By noon we had sold about everything on the tables—which sent us scrambling through the house in search of more junk to sell. That's when I happened upon an old macrame owl. It was tattered, and one eye was missing. Feeling embarrassed to display it, I marked it 25 cents and put it on the back of the table."

"Did it sell?" I asked.

"That afternoon two women spotted it at the same time. The first lady said, 'I'll buy that owl.'

"The second lady protested, 'I saw it first; I'm buying it.'

"'I'll pay 50 cents,' snipped the first lady.

"'Seventy-five cents,' countered the second.

"'One dollar!'

"'Two dollars!'"

Do you know what the owl sold for? . . . One million dollars!

I'm kidding, of course (that's the way the story is supposed to end!). It did, however, go for 10 times its original price. Why? Because some clutteraholic invested two and a half bucks—which means it's worth $2.50. (I wouldn't have paid Monopoly money for it.)

What a Saviour!

In the same way, your value does not result from your performance, possessions, or position. Rather, your value is anchored in what God was willing to pay for you at Calvary.

So next time you feel worthless, consider this prescription: Stand in the shadow of the cross. Gaze upon your Saviour who counts you as more valuable than His own life. And revel in your worth. No matter how poor you feel when you approach the cross, you cannot walk away and wonder if you matter. The cross screams from every splinter: "You matter to the Father."

"You were bought, but not with something that ruins like gold or silver. You were bought with the precious blood of the death of Christ, who was like a pure and perfect lamb" (1 Peter 1:18, 19, ICB).

 # God's Copyright

I wish I could sing like Steven Curtis Chapman. The last time I sang around the house, my canary threw itself to the cat.

I wish I had the hair of Fabio. Actually, I wish I had hair.

I wish I had the triceps and biceps of Arnold Schwarzenegger. All I got is flabby bottomceps.

In my opinion, Jim Carrey's got the life. Wouldn't it be nice to make millions by acting dumb and dumber? Or Barney. Why should a pregnant prune be a national hero? Or David Hasselhoff. Who wouldn't want to live on Baywatch?

I wouldn't mind having a stare like Clint Eastwood's, a smile like Tom Cruise's, and a brain like Johnnie Cochran's. But I don't. I have my eyes. My smile. My muscles. My voice. My brains. My hair (barely).

There will always be people who are richer, smarter, taller, and stronger than I am. But if I waste my life focusing on the things I don't have, I'll never fully appreciate the things I do have.

I'm the only me in the world. And you're the only you. Each of us is uniquely designed by God's hand. He's filed a copyright on every child. We make the best you and me there is.

"I wish that all men were as I am. But each man has his own gift from God; one has this gift, another has that" (1 Cor. 7:7).

Sporting Significance

I love sports. Where else do you get a chance to boo a whole slew of millionaires to their faces?

But not only do I love to watch sports, I love to play. Unfortunately, I'm as coordinated as an elephant on a unicycle. Nonetheless, I've dabbled in most every sport from skiing to parasailing.

Skiing

Skiing looked easy. At least my cousin Danny made it sound that way. "All you got to do," he said, "is strap these waxed boards to your feet and point the tips down the mountain."

Although I couldn't see the sense in paying an arm and a leg to break an arm and a leg, I listened to Danny anyway. "It's a no-brainer," he said. "Anybody with an IQ higher than a jar of mustard can ski."

I shuffled in the lift line with the confidence of a weenie in the Super Bowl. Unfortunately, I moved faster than the line. Are you familiar with the domino theory? A few minutes later I squeaked from the bottom of the pile of skiers, "Who fell?"

Once I made it on the lift, another frightful thought hit me: *Where does this thing go?* I couldn't see where the chairlift ended. For all I knew, it escorted people to the edge of the world—never to be seen again.

Getting off the ski lift wasn't any easier. How was I to know I was supposed to get off *before* the chair curled to reverse direction? (I guess that's where the mustard-level IQ comes in.) Unfortunately, an astute lift attendant noticed I was safely heading down the mountain and alertly stopped the chairs and commanded, "Jump."

"Jump?" I echoed in disbelief. "Get me a bungee cord and we'll talk."

"Jump! Now!"

I slid to the edge of my seat. Closing my eyes, I lunged forward and dropped like a shot duck and landed in front of a sign displaying a large black diamond with the name of the run: "The Devil's Vomit." I peered over the edge like a cat wanting off the roof of the Trump Tower. The ski lodge looked five states away.

Three hours later I was 30 feet down the mountain— only because I was wearing slippery clothing. Eventually I did make it to the bottom, but not gracefully. Are you familiar with the snowball theory? I rolled down the mountain like an avalanche. My shrieks alerted 99 skiers in my way that unless they wanted to take their next run in a wheelchair, they had best stay clear.

As I was bombing toward the ski lodge at Mach 2, a minor question crept into my head: *How does one stop?* It was then I discovered the reason for trees along ski runs. I concluded that skiing is not my spiritual gift. So I thought I'd try an easier sport: parasailing.

Parasailing

"You parasail ever?" the man asked in broken English.

"No," I said as he strapped me into a contraption that looked like the skeleton of a full-body diaper. "But it doesn't look too hard."

"When boat goes, you . . ." the Mexican rambled on in a language I barely understood.

My mind drifted as I gazed at the white beaches of Acapulco. "Now, senor, red flag vairdy, vairdy important, means . . ."

The Gospel According to Platypus

I flinched a bit as he tightened the strap against my sunburn.

"And dis white flag when I wave is . . ."

Breathing deeply, I savored the salty aroma.

"Dat's it," the Mexican screamed to the boat driver as I was whisked off my feet.

Faster than I could say "adios, amigos," I was floating 300 feet above the water. "Yeeeeehaaaaaw," I yelled. I was having more fun than a flea at a dog show. Until the landing.

As the boat circled around I descended toward the guy who was frantically waving his red flag. I struggled to remember what he had said about that flag. Although I could vaguely recall him saying it was "vairdy important," I couldn't remember what it meant.

Suddenly I plummeted toward a beach hut with the speed of a scud missile. Tourists below scurried as if a small asteroid were about to blast a crater on the beach. The man with the flag was screaming expletives at me.

I kept drifting starboard (right) toward the beach hut ("Dagaberto's Delicious Drinks"). I crashed into it, smashing margaritas that instantly belonged to me ($37.83). Fortunately, besides a scolding ("you never parasail here again!"), all I got was a bruise larger than my skin surface area.

Oh yeah—I also got a chance to wonder why a klutz like me would bother with sports.

Why Bother?

I suspect the force fueling our obsession is the need within every human spirit to feel significant. To make a difference at the buzzer. To frolic in the admiration of onlookers. To be part of a team. To excel. To win.

While sports can have value in a Christian's life, no

athletic achievement will really satisfy his or her deeper need. The real issue is how we try to fulfill this more profound quest to feel significant. Some serve the soccer god in hopes of fulfilling it. Others worship the god of skiing. Or the bowling god. They operate under the delusion that a smoother run through the moguls or a higher bowling average will result in greater significance.

Young people of wisdom, however, find significance in God. Authentic, lasting significance has its roots in Christ. Jesus said, "I am the vine; you are the branches. If a man remains in me and I in him, he will bear much fruit; apart from me you can do nothing" (John 15:5). That is to say, we cannot find significance apart from Christ. Only when we submit everything to God's agenda can we actually satisfy our greatest need.

Perspectives on Self-esteem

"If the value of an article is dependent upon the price paid for it, Christ's death made our value skyrocket. Let no one say we are worthless. God is not a foolish speculator; He would never invest in worthless property."—Erwin Lutzer.

"Then Jesus said to his disciples, 'If anyone would come after me, he must deny himself and take up his cross and follow me. For whoever wants to save his life will lose it, but whoever loses his life for me will find it.'"— Matthew 16:24, 25.

"If you have anything really valuable to contribute to the world it will come through the expression of your own personality, that single spark of divinity that sets you off and makes you different from every other living creature."—Bruce Barton.

"You made me and formed me with your hands. Give me understanding so I can learn your commands."—Psalm 119:73, EB.

"He who knows himself best esteems himself least."—H. G. Bohn.

"Do not attempt to do a thing unless you are sure of yourself; but do not relinquish it simply because someone else is not sure of you."—Stewart E. White.

"Very rarely will anyone die for a righteous man, though for a good man someone might possibly dare to die. But God demonstrates his own love for us in this: While we were still sinners, Christ died for us."—Romans 5:7, 8.

"You've no idea what a poor opinion I have of myself—and how little I deserve it."—W. S. Gilbert.

"Self-respect cannot be hunted. It cannot be purchased. It is never for sale. It cannot be fabricated out of public relations. It comes to us when we are alone, in quiet moments, in quiet places, when we suddenly realize that, knowing the good, we have done it; knowing the beautiful, we have served it; knowing the truth, we have spoken it."—Alfred Whitney Griswold.

"A man has to live with himself. He should see to it that he always has good company."—Charles Evans Hughes.

The Gospel
According to Steroids

Tired of Being a Weenie?

It wasn't easy being a fifth grader with a body as brawny as an X-ray. My arm muscles were oversized mosquito bites, my legs like pick-up sticks, and my chest as flat as formica.

Then I noticed an ad that would change my physique forever—so I hoped—tucked in the classifieds near the back of *Hockey Illustrated.*

"Tired of being a weenie?" the ad questioned. "Are you fed up with being pushed around? Sport the muscles of Mr. Atlas! Snag the woman of your dreams. This secret weapon to eternal health is guaranteed, or your money back! Send only $19.95 to: Muscles, P.O. Box 44462, Livingston, NJ 07039."

That's it! I thought. *I can see it now. Women coddling my biceps! Jocks asking for tips on bulking up the quads. Hosting my own TV show*—Mr. Health's Aerobic Hour!

Faster than a dropping dumbbell I ordered the secret weapon.

Muscle Machine

At last the package arrived in the mail. I ripped into

it like a kid at Christmas. As it dropped to the floor, I stared in shock.

Four long silver springs, with red handles on both ends. That's all it was.

But it's all I had. So every night I tugged and yanked and pulled and grunted. I had so many aches and pains, any new ones got put on a weeklong waiting list before I even felt them.

A month slipped by. Nobody accused me of taking steroids. Nobody dubbed me Mr. Atlas. Nobody called me Mr. Health.

But I could feel a difference. Oh, it wasn't a visible transformation. My pecs and quads stayed cartoonish. But inside I felt a trifle stronger. A bit more hearty. Like I was growing—albeit ever so slowly.

Which is precisely the nature of growth, isn't it? Physical, mental, or spiritual—it's gradual. And imperceptible. And arduous.

We wish it weren't so. Desperately we want to believe in a steroids gospel that promises overnight transformation. Muscles in a month. Genius in a day. Spiritual maturity in a week. We send in our bucks on a prayer that perhaps this will be different—only to be reminded that there's no shortcut to growth.

That's why God's advertisement rings different. "Grow up in every way into him who is the head, into Christ, from whom the whole body, joined and knit together by every joint with which it is supplied, when each part is working properly, makes bodily growth and upbuilds itself in love" (Eph. 4:15, 16, RSV).

No quick-fix solution. No overnight change into Super-Christian. Just the gospel truth about how we grow: focus on Christ to mature in love.

The Leprosy Lawn

Last summer I discovered the secret to a lush lawn—fertilizer. My yard belonged in a 12-step group for it was, without question, chemically dependent. The drugs made it look like the eighteenth fairway at Augusta.

Discovering this secret to a green lawn made me as cocky as a farmer in a fruit market. Since I knew the secret, I stopped asking advice. Ignoring the landscaper's counsel on the brand and timing and amount of fertilizer, I loaded up on the cheapest stuff and paid no attention to the proportions suggested for optimum results.

After three weeks of waiting to borrow a friend's spreader, my patience was thinning and my lawn was dying. When I finally got the spreader, it didn't work. Frustrated with the delay and anxious to fertilize before vacation, I ripped into the bags of Fred Meyer's Lawn Food and started throwing the granules everywhere.

What harm could fertilizer do? I wondered. *This is the only way to get green grass fast, so just do it!*

After vacation I was eager to see my yard. Until I saw it.

Staring in disbelief, I started quivering, then sweating. "Honey, tell me it's not so," I mumbled to my wife.

"How embarrassing," she replied in shock. "How did that happen?"

"A comet?" I offered. "Or vandals? Or maybe the fertilizer."

Have you ever seen a lawn with leprosy? If not, come visit me. Splotches of plush green grass are accented with brown desolations the size of Houston. Interspersed between are half-moons that advertise my technique of spreading fertilizer.

I'd Rather Kiss a Catfish

A $143 water bill, a $52 aeration fee, three months of pampering, and my lawn is still as ugly as homemade soup! And there is no hope for recovery—apart from time. Eventually, with the TLC reserved for the White House grounds, my lawn will return to it's former lush fertility. But not by tomorrow. Or the next day. Lawns are governed by the laws of the farm, and one cannot skip or hurry the natural process.

Often we're impatient with the law of the farm. We don't want to resign ourselves to the natural laws that determine the harvest. Instead, we want shortcuts. We expect instant pudding, minute rice, and one-step cameras. Waiting longer than 30 seconds for a seven-layer burrito at Taco Bell sends us into a hissy. Who has time and patience for the law of the farm?

So we try to cheat the system and still win. For example, do you ever goof off through the semester then study all night before a final, trying to cram 12 weeks of study into 12 hours?

Cramming may work in school but not on the farm. Can you imagine playing at the swimming hole all summer, then planting a zillion pumpkin seeds in September, hoping for a harvest overnight? Don't count on any pumpkin pies.

Like it or not, the law of the farm governs every arena of life. What you sow, you reap. So where are you living?

The Farm	The School
Character	
Absolute integrity	A little cheating won't hurt
Compassion to everyone	Compassion when there's something in it for me
Discipline to delay gratification	If it feels good now, do it!

The Gospel According to Steroids

Physical health

Daily, physical exercise	Exercise in PE class
Low fat, high carbohydrates	Twinkies, root beer, and Pringles.
Consistent healthy sleeping patterns	Skip a nights sleep to cram if necessary

Friendships

Others-centered	Self-centered
Insisting on truth even when uncomfortable	Peace-keeping is more important than truth-telling
Forgiveness	Hold grudges

**"Remember this: Whoever sows sparingly will also reap sparingly, and whoever sows generously will also reap generously"
(2 Cor. 9:6).**

The Wise and Foolish Baby-sitters

Want to get rich quick? Just start a baby-sitting business in San Bambino, California. That's all it takes—at least that's what Sandy and Raquel thought.

"With all the babies in this city," Sandy explained, "we could make trillions of dollars just by baby-sitting!"

"No kidding!" her friend Raquel agreed. "Kids are everywhere around here—short kids, fat kids, tall kids, funny kids, funny-looking kids. Kids, kids, kids!"

"I say we start a baby-sitting business," Sandy suggested.

"Great idea!" Raquel agreed.

Unfortunately, that was *all* the two could agree on. On the one hand, Raquel wanted a simple baby-sitting business that offered kids the basics. On the other hand, Sandy conceived of a service that would appeal to the wild side of kids.

"Let's build a party palace where babies can dance their pampers off," Sandy exclaimed. "We've got to appeal to the sensationalism in kids."

"I dunno," Raquel sheepishly challenged. "I don't think the parents will go for that."

"Bag the parents! We'll blast 'em outta the place with rock and roll. Parents won't even be allowed in the building."

Still trying to mend their differences, Raquel replied, "But that's not good for kids. Don't you think we ought to build the business on such principles as integrity, discipline and good things, and stuff like that?"

"Is your head full of sawdust or what?" Sandy

retorted. "That's not what kids like. Forget honesty and discipline and all that junk. Party! That's what kids want."

"But that's not good for . . ."

"Who cares? We'll make lots of money 'cuz that's what sells—parties, games, and rock 'n' roll."

"But couldn't we just play, um, well, you know, baby music like 'Rock-a-bye Baby'?"

"You're soooooooooooooooooo old-fashioned! It's gonna be rock 'n' roll in my center."

"Not in mine!" Raquel determined. "It's going to be 'Rock-a-bye Baby.'"

And so the "best friends" parted company. Each girl determined to create the greatest baby-sitting business in San Bambino.

Under Construction

Raquel invested in a plot of land in the downtown district. Determined to follow all the rules to assure the building would be safe and secure, she worked her way through all the red tape with the city council to obtain the necessary building permits. She debated with the SSSBLB—Society to Save San Bambino's Lands for the Bambinos—for the right to develop the growing downtown district. And she negotiated with building contractors to construct a facility on a rock-solid foundation.

Finally, the sign was hoisted in place. It flashed above the city street—"A Better Day Care."

Meanwhile, Sandy started her own baby-sitting empire. "Why build downtown?" she mused to herself. "I want to be where the parties are." So she began construction on the beach.

"Whatcha building there, young lady?" an old man interrupted her work one day.

"Oh, I'm building a day-care center so I can baby-sit kids," she replied. "I'm going to call it The Kids' Wild Kingdom. I suspect someday it will be a national franchise."

"But don'tcha think you may need a buildin' permit?"

"Nah, that's just for downtown construction, I think. Anyway, I ain't got time to mess with that nonsense. I want to get rich quick."

"But don'tcha need a foundation? Somehow that sand don't look solid enough to just slap a building on it like you're doing."

"You're just old-fashioned," Sandy replied. "Besides, kids won't know the difference. My customers won't care about the foundation."

"Whatever you say," the old man shrugged as he continued on his way.

The Wise Have It

A few days later The Kids' Wild Kingdom opened for business. It bedazzled the senses! Neon lights flashed. Mirror balls swirled. Rock music blasted. Balloons punctuated the party atmosphere.

It offered all the latest conveniences: a drive-through for parents to drop off their kids; the world's largest sand-box; drinking fountains that spouted root beer instead of water; and of course, a petting farm known as Fuzzy Strokes for Little Folks.

In The Kids' Wild Kingdom the kids had no rules. They were free to say, do, and try anything. Kids went wherever they wanted. Total freedom was the only concern.

Raquel and Sandy were now competitors. The "best friends" rarely heard from each other. Occasionally Raquel would see the pictures of some of Sandy's clients on the back of milk cartons, but for the most part they continued with life as usual.

And then it happened. Suddenly. Dramatically. What all Californians fear most. It was "the big one"! An earthquake that rattled San Bambino like popcorn in a popper. The earth rumbled. Bridges collapsed. Buildings toppled.

KSBN's newscaster, Tom Brokeoff, reported the catastrophe to America. Newspaper reporters scurried about the rubble. Sirens screamed up and down the streets.

In the aftermath of the disaster Raquel and Sandy assessed the damage. Although both girls wanted to get rich quick, only one succeeded.

A Better Day Care stood like a mighty sequoia in a mild breeze. Oh, there was a picture that fell and a glass bottle that shattered, but nothing to report to the All-Shake Insurance Company. Suddenly Raquel had more business than she could handle. The babies kept crawling in, and she never missed a beat singing "Rock-a-bye Baby."

The Kids' Wild Kingdom, on the other hand, was decimated. When the earth shook, the building did fall, and down came The Kingdom, cradles, and all.

"Therefore everyone who hears these words of mine and puts them into practice is like a wise man who built his house on the rock. The rain came down, the streams rose, and the winds blew and beat against that house; yet it did not fall, because it had its foundation on the rock. But everyone who hears these words of mine and does not put them into practice is like a foolish man who built his house on sand.

The rain came down, the streams rose, and
the winds blew and beat against that house,
and it fell with a great crash"
(Matt. 7:24-27).

Hedging the Bet for Victory

January 24, 1994.

Here I sit. The smoke swirls. The lights flash. The coins jingle. The siren screams. The winners squeal. The liquor flows.

I feel the gush of adrenaline surging as I soak in the electric atmosphere. A Samoan woman decked in pearls and red velvet wails, "You're so vain, I bet you think this . . ."

An attendant scurries past me in her starchy white blouse and sheen bow tie. A pit boss scowls as his eyes dart from table to table. A police officer eyes me suspiciously as I sit here with my journal.

Nevada Crossing Hotel and Casino. It's an enticing place to stay on my way to Sacramento. My supper cost me all of two bucks. The amenities (Jacuzzi, pool, and five Andes chocolate mints on my pillow) are ample. All for a mere $24.95 a night. It's a traveler's dream—except for the lobby.

To get to your room or the registration desk or the public restrooms or the restaurant or the pool or *anywhere*—you have to cross the lobby. It's a jungle of dizzying lights, swirling mirror balls, and chanting craps dealers.

So here I sit in the lobby, reflecting. About the glitz of sin. About the pull of temptation. About the similarities between Nevada Crossing Casino and the world.

Sucked In

The lure is so magnetic. The tentacles so long. God, how can we not be sucked in? How do we grow into Your likeness in a world like this?

Satan must be laughing and Jesus crying over priorities gone askew. Over our trashed lives. Over the human race so hoodwinked by the prince of darkness in this palace of lights.

Absent are the stories of marriages shattered by the gambling addiction. No one here tells of the child at home wondering where Daddy is tonight. I seem to be the only one here thinking of how all this money could feed a thousand orphans in Somalia.

And the insanity snowballs.

O God, how do we gain victory in a world so seductive?

And I hear His voice whisper over the ringing slot machines, "For God sent not his Son into the world to condemn the world; but that the world through him might be saved" (John 3:17).

Thank You, God. Thank You.

The Indwelling Spirit of Buttermilk

A man who drank heavily was converted to Christ and lived victoriously for several weeks. One day as he passed the open door of a tavern, the pungent odor drifting out aroused his old appetite for liquor. Just then he saw a sign in the window of a nearby cafe: "All the buttermilk you can drink—25 cents!" Dashing inside, he ordered one glass, then another, and still another. After finishing the third he walked past the saloon and was no longer tempted. Full of buttermilk, he had no room for anything else. The lesson is clear: to be victorious over our evil desires, we must leave no opportunity for them to repossess us.

Dwight L. Moody once demonstrated the principle like this: "Tell me," he said to his audience, "how can I get the air out of the tumbler I have in my hand?"

One man suggested, "Suck it out with a pump."

But the evangelist replied, "That would create a vacuum and shatter it." After many suggestions, Moody picked up a pitcher and quietly filled the glass with water. "There," he said, "all the air is now removed." He then explained that victory for the child of God does not come by working hard to eliminate sinful habits, but rather by allowing the Holy Spirit to take full possession. When the Spirit invades, Jesus promised that "he will guide you into all truth."

Perspectives on Growth

"Everybody thinks of changing humanity and nobody thinks of changing himself."—Leo Tolstoy.

"Like newborn babies, crave pure spiritual milk, so that by it you may grow up in your salvation."—1 Peter 2:2.

"Once someone came upon Michelangelo chipping away his chisel at a huge shapeless piece of rock. He asked the sculptor what he was doing. 'I am releasing the angel imprisoned in this marble,' he answered. Jesus is the one who sees and can release the hidden hero in every man."—William Barclay.

"When change is successful we look back at it and call it growth!"—John Maxwell.

High in the Alps is a monument raised in honor of a faithful guide who perished while ascending a peak to rescue a stranded tourist. Inscribed on that memorial stone are these words: "He Died Climbing." A maturing, growing Christian should have the same kind of attitude, right up to the end of life.

"In fact, though by this time you ought to be teachers, you need someone to teach you the elementary truths of God's word all over again. You need milk, not solid food! Anyone who lives on milk, being still an infant, is not acquainted with the teaching about righteousness. But solid food is for the mature, who by constant use have trained themselves to distinguish good from evil."—Hebrews 5:12-14.

"There are some Christians whose spiritual bodies are atrophied and squat. They're still at the milk and pabulum stage, when they should be digesting steak and potatoes. And their spiritual "muscle" is correspondingly misshaped—appearing more like a Barbie doll's than the Incredible Hulk's."— S. Rickly Christian.

"Being a Christian is more than just an instantaneous conversion—it is a daily process whereby you grow to be more and more like Christ. Jesus Christ is the man God wants every man to be like."—Billy Graham.

"The fact is, Christians are more to blame for not being revived than sinners are for not being converted."—Charles Finney.

"If you don't live it, you don't believe it."—Paul Harvey.

The Gospel
According to Fuzzies

 The Fuzzy File

I pull it out whenever I feel a few curves short of a smiley face. When Tattoo Harley flips me an obscene gesture on the interstate (he was camping in my blind spot). When Saint Angelica snubs me for eating Peppermint Patties (she prefers "tofu patties"). When Puritan Priscilla snubs other nationalities ("If you ain't Dutch, you ain't much"). That's when I pull out my "warm fuzzy file."

Want to see it? It's a collection of torn notes and faded letters. Some of them date back to the days when I had hair on my head and none on my legs. (That's a long time ago!) The file isn't much, but it's a Power Bar to a bruised spirit. Take a peek:

From a college professor:
Dear Karl,
There are some occasions that come along that make a preaching teacher proud, even if he must admit he has had very little to do with the end result. Such an occasion was the memorial service on Tuesday. Your presentation

simply could not have been more appropriate for the occasion. In addition, it was delivered with perfection. If I were still grading you, the grade would have to be an A+.

From a church member:
Dear Karl,
    Thank you for changing my life.

From the students at Shenandoah Valley Academy:
Dear Karl,
    Your presence here on this campus has been a true blessing for all of us. Your brilliant and witty stories have uplifted us and made us realize that Christianity can be fun. You have also helped us understand that God's love is unconditional and ever-accepting.

If you aren't collecting warm fuzzies, then start today. They're as refreshing as Peppermint Patties.
    And if you aren't giving warm fuzzies, also begin today. They're as healthy as tofu patties!

"But encourage one another daily, as long as it is called Today, so that none of you may be hardened by sin's deceitfulness" (Heb. 3:13).

An Encouraging Word (or Two or Three or more)

Yes.
I'll call you.
Please forgive me.
There are seconds on dessert.
Where did you find that adorable skirt?
Tell me about it.
The audit shows the IRS owes you money.
Free.
Great job.
I love you.
You've been accepted.
What song would you like to hear?
The test is canceled.
Could you use a raise?
You get a second chance.
Fat-free.
The forecast calls for sunshine.
No cavities.
I couldn't have done it without you.
Nice haircut.
God bless you.
No problem.
What do you think?
It was the spark plugs, not the transmission.
I heard she really likes you.
You are in my prayers.

"Pleasant words are a honeycomb, sweet to
the soul and healing to the bones"
(Prov. 16:24).

Bringing Out the Best in Others

He looked like a ballerina playing in the Super Bowl. In contrast to the other giants, he was short, slow, and white.

"Look at that guy wearing number 1. What's he doing in the NBA?" I asked.

"I was just watching him too," my buddy Mark replied.

In our quest to visit every arena in the National Basketball Association, never had we seen an athlete who looked more displaced. He appeared as athletic as Rush Limbaugh. But he had the heart of Forrest Gump.

"Probably a star in a no-name college, but never here in the big leagues," Mark said.

"Yeah," I stared as he rifled brick after brick toward the rim. "Look! The ball boys throw four warm-up balls to Hakeem for every one they throw to Blondie."

"I bet you can count his total minutes played this season on no hands."

Show time

Without warning, the arena lights dimmed as the athletes scurried off the court. "And now, ladies and gentlemen," the announcer blared, "introducing the starting lineup for the 1994 world champion Houuuuuuuuuuuuuuuuuuuuuuuuuuuuuuston Rockets!"

The deafening beat of Queen blasted, "We will . . . we will . . . rock you!" The cheerleaders danced as if they had overdosed on No Doz. Fireworks exploded. Fans went ballistic. The starters galloped through a tunnel of metallic-red pom-poms. "Let the showdown at the Summit begin!"

Blondie plopped on the bench with the other reserves. Appearing as comfortable with his role as a slug in a puddle, he cheered the dunks. And whined the miscalls. And high-fived his winded teammates. But he never broke a sweat.

The game unfolded as expected. The Rockets made the Minnesota Timberwolves look like a pickup team at church.

Fans were more interested in the departure of Dusty Hill (lead singer and bass guitarist for ZZ Top) than in the blowout. Hill signed autographs and posed with pushy fans as he moseyed from center court toward the exit. All eyes seemed riveted on his two-foot-long beard. Until Blondie stepped on the court.

Blondiemania

With 3 minutes and 11 seconds remaining in the game, the announcer said, "Now playing for the Houston Rockets, number 1, Scott Brooks."

Somehow that announcement breathed new excitement into the 34-point massacre. Apparently Mark and I were not the only fans who noticed the underdog.

"That guy never plays," quipped the season ticket holder next to Mark. "When he touches the ball, you *know* the game is over."

Although the game was over, the excitement wasn't. The crowd erupted in cheers whenever Brooks dribbled the ball. "Shoot, shoot, shoot . . ." a choir of fans chanted.

As if to fulfill his destiny, Brooks fired a shot—an air ball that didn't get much closer to the rim than the scorekeepers. "Ooooooooooooooooooooooooooh," the audience collectively sighed. Undaunted by his failure, the chanting continued. "Shoot, Scottie, shoot! Shoot, Scottie, shoot!"

Again, Brooks launched a prayer toward the net that clanged off the front of the rim. But the crowd persisted. "Scott-eeeee! Scott-eeeee! Scott-eeeee!"

With 13 seconds remaining, Scott Brooks got one more chance—a 15-foot jump shot from the side. The ball sailed toward the hoop and kissed nothing but the bottom of the net!

The audience erupted. You'd have thought that either the Beatles had reunited or the president had canceled all taxes. "Scott-eeeee! Scott-eeeee! Scott-eeeee!" Playing to a standing ovation, Scott Brooks danced at center court—his arms flung heavenward like Rocky after a knockout punch.

Give It a Shot

A boring game with a brilliant ending it was. Brilliant because the underdog barked. The no-name made a name. The sap scored.

And we all felt as though we had lent a finger to that final swish. We helped write that story for Blondie to tell his grandkids someday. As we supported, he sparkled.

Which makes me ponder: Why not encourage more often? Why not invest more of myself in bringing out the best in others?

So give it a shot today. High-five your best friend's new romance. Support your dad's dream of earning a new degree. Be your teacher's biggest cheerleader. Gamble a compliment or two.

"Therefore encourage one another and build each other up" (1 Thess. 5:11). It makes the game more fun—for everybody.

Kissy Prissy and the Gospel

Creating poodles had to be a mistake. Call me politically incorrect, picket my house with posters, sue me—I still hate poodles. OK—"hate" is too strong. Let's say I can't *understand* them.

For starters, I can't understand what they are. They're not dogs. Dogs run. Poodles tiptoe for fear of breaking a nail. Dogs scratch and sniff in inappropriate places. Poodles expect you to do that for them. Dogs crave steaks. Poodles prefer caviar. No, the poodle is not a dog. A bizarre blend of ET, the Lucky Charms leprechaun, a Chia Pet, and the Energizer Bunny maybe, but a dog the poodle is not.

Second, I can't understand how they survive. Could you last in a world in which everyone called you Fifi or Sissy or Lambchop? How would you like to be cursed with manicured toenails, ribbons, and a haircut weird enough to make Dennis Rodman blush? Seems to me that "the survival of the fittest" law would have kicked in long before now. But for some inexplicable reason, poodles still yap. Which brings me to my final point.

I can't understand why poodles won't SHUUUUUUUT UUUUUUUUUP! A poodle sees the same mail carrier every day at the same time for 30 years. But when letters arrive, you'd swear it was the Second Coming. Every poodle in the world feels responsible for proclaiming the appearance of junk mail.

Poodles are the strongest argument I've heard for why animals should be spayed.

Face-to-Face With a Monster

Maybe I'm overreacting. Recently I found myself molested by a certain "Prissy the Poodle." She clamored all over me while the owner cooed, "That's like sooooooooooooooooo adorably cute! Prissy, keep slobbering on Karl's cheek. I'll get my camera!"

So I closed my eyes. And wrinkled my face. And extended my hand to pet the monster rat.

And you know what? I discovered poodles respond to a gentle touch just like any other dog. As I stroked her curly fur, Prissy purred like a cat. And since my eyes were closed, she seemed as warm and cuddly as any other dog.

Lately I've encountered human poodles, too. They can't figure out who they are. Barking about their abuse, they get in your face for attention and become as irritating as static on the radio.

But you know what? When I reach out and embrace them, they respond like every other human. Their heart purrs and their spirit sings. It's not always easy to endure their slobber, but it is always Christ-honoring.

And who knows? With enough practice, maybe someday I'll embrace them as Christ did—with eyes wide open.

"But the fruit of the Spirit is love" (Gal. 5:22).

 # Heroes 101

"In first grade Mr. Lohr said my purple teepee wasn't realistic enough, that purple was no color for a tent, that purple was a color for people who died, and that my drawing wasn't good enough to hang with the others. I walked back to my seat counting the swish-swish-swish of my baggy corduroy trousers. With a black crayon, nightfall came to my purple tent in the middle of an afternoon.

"In second grade Mr. Barta said, 'Draw anything.' He didn't care what. I left my paper blank and when he came around to my desk, my heart beat like a tom-tom while he touched my head with his big hand and in a soft voice said, 'The snowfall. How clean and white and beautiful.'"

Teachers such as Mr. Barta should be applauded. Sorry, Michael Jordan, Tom Hanks, Sir Mixalot, but I think teachers are the real heroes today. They ignite our confidence. And hoist our dreams. And stretch our minds.

I've had some Mr. Bartas in my life. If you don't mind, I'd like to drop them a thank-you note. You're welcome to read the letters under one condition—you promise to send a letter today to the "Mr. Barta" in your life.

~ ~ ~

"Dear Mr. Rice (fifth-and sixth-grade teacher, Cedar Brook School, Rehoboth, Massachusetts),

"I've still got a Kidsville dollar that I earned for my science project. (Had I invested it, I would own the Kidsville store by now!) And every now and then I recall how you'd occasionally interrupt history class with 'Plaaaaaay ball!' (Sorry, I can't remember the history lessons.) And I can't see an airplane without thinking of the time you let me land your Cessna (I was 12 years old—what were you thinking?).

"Bob, you made school a carnival. Your explosive laughter, your energetic song service, your peanut butter pancakes, your 'surprise package,' your stories about Jesus—all of these 'Bobisms' rank as my most enjoyable memories of school. Thank you. You'll always be my hero."

~ ~ ~

"Dear Mrs. Liers (algebra and geometry teacher, Shenandoah Valley Academy, New Market, Virginia),

"Math came about as naturally to me as childbirth. But your infectious smile and encouraging word spurred me on when I wanted to quit.

"I remember a little of your math—mostly the Pythagorean theorem (because you let Kevin, Jim, and me teach that day). But I remember a lot about you. I remember you were the only teacher who noticed I was squinting to see the board. Then you helped me adjust to the trauma of being called 'four-eyes.' I remember the time you said my sermon at the student week of prayer was 'the finest I've ever heard from anybody.' And I remember the day you hugged me when I bombed one of your quizzes. Thanks for the memories."

~ ~ ~

"Dear Dr. Bursey (professor of theology, Walla Walla College, College Place, Washington),

"Sitting in your class was the closest I'll ever come on this earth to feeling as if I'm sitting on a hillside listening to Jesus. That's why I audited your classes when I couldn't take them for credit.

"I remember you saying, 'You can't spend an hour

with Jesus and remain the same person.' I learned that I couldn't spend an hour in your class and not feel as though I had been with Jesus. Thank you."

"Anyone who receives instruction in the word must share all good things with his instructor" (Gal. 6:6).

Perspectives on Encouragement

"It is critical not to be critical."—Martha Bolton.

"One of the highest of human duties is the duty of encouragement. It is easy to pour cold water on their enthusiasm; it is easy to discourage others. The world is full of discouragers. We have a Christian duty to encourage one another. Many a time a word of praise or thanks or appreciation or cheer has kept a man on his feet."—William Barclay.

"Kindness is a language the dumb can speak and the deaf can hear and understand."—Christian Nestell Bovee.

"The tongue that brings healing is a tree of life"—Proverbs 15:4.

Allan Emery had an experience that made a deep impression upon him. His father received a call saying a well-known Christian had been found at a certain place drunk on the sidewalk. Immediately his father sent his chauffeured limousine to pick the man up, while his mother prepared the best guest room. Allan watched, wide-eyed, as the beautiful coverlets were turned down on the exquisite old four-poster bed, revealing the monogrammed sheets.

"But Mother," he protested, "he's drunk. He might even get sick."

"I know," his mother replied kindly, "but this man has slipped and fallen. When he comes to, he will be so ashamed. He will need all the loving encouragement we can give him."

It was a lesson the son never forgot.

"You can always tell a real friend by the fact that when you've made a fool of yourself he doesn't feel you've done a permanent job."—Lawrence Peters.

"And let us consider how we may spur one another on toward love and good deeds" (Heb. 10:24).

The Gospel
According to Manure

The Gospel
According to Manure

Why do we spend $5 on church-related buildings for every dollar we spend on evangelistic activity? Does this honor the One who told us that He does not live in houses made by people? What would happen if we spent that money on AIDS hospices or halfway houses for prison inmates or homes for the poor?

Such questions haunt me. It's not that I'm against church buildings; it's just that I can't believe God called us to hole up in plush sanctuaries while the world slides toward hell. Doesn't it seem strange that we discuss wedding bands while researchers project that 120 million people will be infected with the AIDS virus by the year 2000? Does it seem odd to you that we squabble about the color of carpet in the toddlers' room while approximately one of three fetuses is aborted? Is it disturbing to hear of church members quibbling that the youth deacon didn't wear a tie while 10 percent of adolescent boys and 18 percent of adolescent girls admit they have attempted suicide?

As a pastor I grapple daily with these issues. Maybe you can understand my sympathy for unchurched friends who scratch their heads when Christians huddle to talk about being the light of the world. The world is infested with Christian talkers. "Theodore Theologian" rambles about glorification, justification, and sanctification. His counterpart, "Reverend Pat Popcorn," howls his holy hype: "Praise Gawd! Jump for joy! Send me money by calling 1-900-I'm-a-sucker! Get your authentic Jerusalem mud! Aaaaaaamen!"

Just to talk Christianese is senseless. James puts it this way: "Show me how anyone can have faith without actions. I will show you my faith by my actions" (James 2:18, TEV). Christian words without action are as valuable as manure.

That's not to say that manure has no potential value. In a big pile it steams and stinks and serves no good. But spread out, it's a potent fertilizer that will make your garden grow faster than a Chia Pet. The gospel of manure is simple: it's valuable when dispersed.

Likewise, our impact as Christians is greatest when we are dispersed. When we infiltrate our polluted world with the healing grace of Jesus, we fulfill our highest calling.

Sharing Christ Without Being a Weirdo

A Hawaiian street preacher glared at me, his breath reeking of onion. His knuckles glowed as he gripped his tattered Bible. "Arrrreeeee yoooooooouuuuuuu saaaaaaaaaved?"

"Well, I, um," I stuttered with the confidence of a mouse at a cat show.

"Judgment is coming. Sin will be destroyed. Are you saved?"

"Um, yes, I am."

His next word I will never forget. His face softened, his voice calmed, and his knuckles relaxed. "OK," he said simply as he left me shaking on Ala Moana Boulevard.

While I admire that man's convictions, I can't help wondering how many people respond favorably to his approach. Personally, I consider it as inviting as a beesting.

Show, Don't Tell

When Jesus talked about God to people He met on the street, He tried to be as understandable as possible. Using parables and sharing stories, He melted their defenses and penetrated their hearts.

Moreover, He didn't just *tell* people about God's love; He *showed* God's love. The cripple saw it. So did the whore. And the leper. Jesus showed us that witnessing means taking personal action, not urging others to do something.

Even Peter, the disciple who usually didn't catch on,

learned Christ's technique of witnessing. He counseled:
"Live such good lives among the pagans that, though they
accuse you of doing wrong, they may see your good deeds
and glorify God on the day he visits us" (1 Peter 2:12).

Let's suppose tomorrow morning you wake up mute—
you can't say a word. If your friends are to discover Jesus,
it will be based on your actions, not your words. How
effective would you be in sharing Christ?

Witnessing in Pain

At first I thought I was dreaming. A week later, I'm still hoping to awaken from the nightmare.

"The paramedics are here." My wife seemed to be in shock.

"Huh? Uh, what?"

"It's Mom. I got up at 5:00 a.m. to feed the baby and, um, she, ah—"

"What happened, Cherié? Tell me."

"Mom, um, said she'd . . . I can't believe this is happening . . . she said she had been up for an hour because she had chest pains. I called 911, and . . . oh, Karl . . . she's always been so healthy . . . what are we going to do? . . . if only I'd . . ."

Through wet eyes I watched the paramedics try to coax life back into her mother. Ambulance lights danced on the ceiling—lulling me into a numb trance. Radios blared an unknown language. Six men scurried like a pit crew. And mom died.

I know this season of pain will not endure forever. But right now it seems as if it will.

Mom's absence leaves a gaping hole. Whom will we run to when life gets messy? Who will baby-sit Lindsey? Who will send the birthday cards? give the Bible studies? cook the Thanksgiving meal? prolong the game of Pit by holding one of every stock? take us to the airport? deliver us home-grown tomatoes? listen? punctuate our lives with sparkle, giggles, and class?

Who will be our "Jesus" now? I don't know.

In the wake of Mom's untimely death, I scramble to cover my commitments. This chapter must be written, even though I don't feel like writing. Life trudges on through the tears that still puddle in my eyes.

Through the chaos Christ's words ring therapeutic: "Greater love has no one than this, that he lay down his life for his friends" (John 15:13).

I've seen a living demonstration of "greater love" his week. Through this season of heartache friends have showed me what the text means by "lay down your life." Here's a couple snapshots.

Bob

Bob didn't say much. He cried a lot. And gave a great hug. Then he said one thing more comforting than any of the cliches: "Can I wash your car so it will be clean when you go to the funeral tomorrow?" When he returned, my Toyota sparkled like a new silver filling.

Ron, Jeanine, Janae, and Jealynn Preast

The Preasts showed up shortly after Mom's death. I was standing in a mountain of boxes feeling overwhelmed. "Is the moving van still coming tomorrow?" Jeanine asked.

"Yeah," I said.

"I guess the timing couldn't be worse, huh? Is everything ready to move?"

"Yeah," I lied.

"Are you sure? Could we scrub your floors? Wrap your sofas? Clean out your freezer?"

"Yes. Yes. Yes."

I stared blankly at the garage walls while they worked like an army of ants. By midnight they had everything ready to move.

It wasn't their words that meant so much—it was their presence. They laid down their lives by rolling up their sleeves.

The response of Christian friends has left us dizzy: prayers on CompuServe, meals provided by the ladies' Bible fellowship, cards, flowers, and a gift certificate to buy Mom's favorite kind of tree for the front yard. Clearly, Christ's love still lives.

And may I state the obvious? Nothing makes Christianity more appealing than Christians who act like Christ. No evangelistic sermon delivers the same punch. No Bible study makes the same impact. No gospel presentation speaks louder than a Christian "laying down their life for a friend."

So whom can you witness to today?

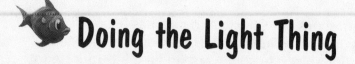

Doing the Light Thing

A long time ago in the mountains of North Korea there lived a woodsman. One day while he was working in the forest a huge tiger attacked him. The woodsman seized the tiger by the tail, and the tiger began turning around in circles, trying to get its teeth into the woodsman. A Buddhist monk, out for a walk and attracted by the noise, sauntered over. The woodsman, upon seeing the monk, cried out, "Please take my ax there and kill this tiger before I am eaten alive."

The monk, lowering his eyes and piously folding his hands, replied, "I am sorry, but I cannot kill the tiger. You see, I am a Buddhist, and as a Buddhist all life is sacred to me, be it insect, human, or animal."

The woodsman answered, "Fortunately, I am not blessed with your belief, so would you please take my place at the tail of the tiger and let me kill the beast?"

The monk agreed, and they exchanged places. The woodsman then walked over, picked up his ax, placed it on his shoulder, and nonchalantly strolled off into the forest. The Buddhist monk, very much alarmed, cried out, "Please, come back and kill this tiger as you promised or else I will be devoured."

The woodsman's parting reply was: "I was so impressed by your example that I have become a convert to your belief."

Buddhism or Christianity

People become converted to Christianity in the same way—by watching our example. That's why Jesus told His followers: "You're here to be light, bringing out the

The Gospel According to Manure

God-colors in the world. God is not a secret to be kept. We're going public with this, as public as a city on a hill. If I make you lightbearers, you don't think I'm going to hide you under a bucket, do you? I'm putting you on a light stand. Now that I've put you there on a hilltop, on a light stand—shine! Keep open house; be generous with your lives. By opening up to others, you'll prompt people to open up with God, this generous Father in heaven" (Matt. 5:14-16. Message).

As Christians we are challenged to radiate with the aura of Jesus. We're called to be 120 watts of Sylvania Soft White in our dark neighborhoods.

In a world full of shadows, sometimes it is difficult to believe that we can make a difference. Sometimes our lights seem small compared to the overwhelming darkness that engulfs us: abortions, carjacking, kidnapping, robberies, graffiti, child molestation, date rape, wife battering, deadbeat dads, porno shops, and crack cocaine.

But take heart—in a thousand dim arenas of need around the world, the light still shines in the darkness—and the darkness cannot extinguish it. The only light some will ever see is the radiance that shines through you and me. So try it today—at home or school, at a barbecue or a Bible study, in Taco Bell or a traffic jam—do the light thing.

I'd Rather Kiss a Catfish

"The day I become a Christian is the day the pope gets married," scoffed an unbeliever. He had as much interest in spiritual matters as Howard Stern and didn't mind using four-letter words to tell you so. Alcohol, fast cars, and fishing consumed his life. His nickname? "Satan's schoolmate."

For 30 years he scoffed at his wife and four kids for going to church. Nonetheless, they prayed for Daddy every day. They tried to lead surrendered lives to influence him for Christ. The invitation came weekly: "Daddy, will you come to church with us today?"

"I'd rather kiss a catfish." His sarcasm left the family with little hope for change.

Perhaps you too are trying to influence someone for Christ. Maybe you hold little hope for change. If so, don't give up. Influencing others is possible provided you use the right method.

The Right Method

A wise old man discovered the method of persuasion that worked for him. He retired in a modest rambler next to a junior high school. Retirement proved to be quiet and peaceful . . . until a new school year began. The next afternoon a posse of boys marched down the street, beating on every trash can they saw. The banging continued day after day, until finally the old man decided to take some action.

The next afternoon he met the young percussionists as they whacked their way along the street. Stopping them, he said, "You boys really know how to make a good

142

racket. I've been noticing your rhythm and can't say I've heard anything better in all my days. I used to play the snare in our high school marching band, but nothing like the sounds you boys put out. Will you do me a favor? I'll give you each a dollar if you'll promise to come around every afternoon and beat the garbage cans."

The kids were delighted and continued to do a bang-up job on the trash cans. After a few days the old man greeted the kids again, but this time a concerned look drooped his face. "This recession has taken a big chunk out of my income," he explained. "From now on, I'll only be able to pay you 50 cents to beat on the cans." The percussionists were displeased, but accepted his offer and continued their afternoon ruckus.

A few days later the sage retiree approached them again. "I hate to break this to you," he said, "but I haven't received my Social Security check yet, so I can pay you only 25 cents. Is that OK?"

"A lousy quarter?" the drum leader exclaimed. "If you think we're going to bust our cans every afternoon for a quarter, you're crazy! Not a chance, mister. We quit!" And the old man enjoyed peace and serenity for the rest of his years.

Using the Right Method

Like I said, influencing others is possible provided you use the right method. The old man discovered his. What about you? What method could possibly win over the heart of a Buddhist girlfriend or a belligerent father?

In Bible times Peter shared an effective method in witnessing and wrote to women who were banging their heads against chariots wondering how they might influence their atheist husbands for Christ. In 1 Peter 3:2-4 he tells them not to attempt to influence their husbands by "the wearing of gold jewelry and fine clothes. Instead, it should be that of your inner self, the unfading beauty of a gentle and quiet spirit, which is of great worth in God's sight."

His method is simple: others find themselves drawn to Christ when they see Christ in you. Every week in church I am reminded of how effective this method is when I greet Satan's-schoolmate-turned-Christian. His typical reply: "Pastor, that sermon was better than any catfish I ever kissed."

Perspectives on Witnessing

"Evangelism is a sharing of gladness."—*Author Unknown.*

"Then Jesus came to them and said, 'All authority in heaven and on earth has been given to me. Therefore go and make disciples of all nations, baptizing them in the name of the Father and of the Son and of the Holy Spirit, and teaching them to obey everything I have commanded you. And surely I am with you always, to the very end of the age.'"—Matthew 28:18-20.

"Evangelism is a very individual thing. It happens when you take personal action, not when you urge others to do something."—S. Rickly Christian.

"Lighthouses don't fire guns or ring bells to call attention to their light; they just shine."—*Author Unknown.*

"When a Christian is winning souls, he isn't messing around with sin."—George L. Smith.

"Far too many Christians have been anesthetized into thinking that if they simply live out their faith in an open and consistent fashion, the people around them will see it, want it, and somehow figure out how to get it for themselves."—Bill Hybels.

"If evangelicals stop trying to convert others, they will be rather lonely, for advertisers, New Age pitch-persons, and advocates of every other therapy and worldview are aggressively making their pitches."—Martin E. Marty.

"One of the saddest statistics of our day is that 95 percent of all church members have never led anyone to Christ."—D. James Kennedy.

"There are two ways of spreading light; to be the candle or the mirror that reflects it."—Edith Wharton.

" 'Come, follow me,' Jesus said, 'and I will make you fishers of men.' "—Matthew 4:19.

"Some people are just waiting for a contagious Christian who won't beat around the bush, but who'll clarify the truth of Christ and challenge them to do something about it. Could that Christian be you?"—Bill Hybels.

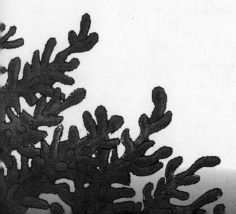

The Gospel
According to Overalls

Religion in Overalls

Recently I heard of a young volunteer who served with Mother Teresa in Calcutta. The first morning as Mother Teresa showed the volunteer around the children's home, they came to a dying baby in a bassinet. The baby had been rescued off the streets, but there was no medical help available to save it.

Mother Teresa cuddled the baby, then handed her to the new volunteer and said, "Do not let this baby die without having been loved."

The volunteer later wrote: "I held that baby in my arms and I loved her until she died at 6:00 in the evening. I spent the hours humming Brahms' 'Lullaby.' And you know, I could feel that baby, as tiny and as weak as she was—I could feel that baby pressing herself against me."

Even a dying infant responds to love. That's because love is our deepest human need.

Love is the core value of the Christian faith. James put it this way: "The Christian who is pure and without fault, from God the Father's point of view, is the one who takes care of orphans and widows" (James 1:27, TLB).

It seems too simple, doesn't it? Love people who are in need—that's the heartbeat of Christianity. No mention of church attendance, stained glass, pews, kneeling, or singing. Instead, Scripture tells us that pure religion means embracing the helpless. It means inviting the fat kid that nobody likes to your birthday party. It means volunteering at the homeless shelter. It means hanging out with the new kid in school who smells funny. It means putting on overalls to help the elderly neighbor weed her rose garden. Pure religion cuts through the churchy motions and addresses the deepest human need—to love and to be loved.

So why not give it a whirl today? You'll be amazed at the response.

The Little Guy Without a Seat

Last night there was more testosterone per square inch in the Kingdome than anywhere else on the planet. Sixty-five thousand men gathered in Seattle to sing songs, hold hands, listen to inspiring speakers, and wait 23 minutes to go to the restroom.

The Christian men's movement is called Promise Keepers. Beginning in 1990 with a core of 72 men, it has exploded into a national phenomenon that now draws a yearly attendance of a half-million men.

The spark plug behind the phenomenon is Bill McCartney, who resigned as head coach of the University of Colorado football team to devote more time to his dream of inspiring men to lead lives of integrity. He is a great man on a great mission.

What impressed me most about Bill McCartney was not his stirring appeal that sparked a 15-minute standing ovation. It wasn't his pep talk that ignited noise so deafening I couldn't hear myself scream. No, what impressed me most about him was an empty chair.

That's right, an empty chair. It wasn't empty for long—this event sold out months ago. But the chair was empty long enough to remind us that true greatness comes in caring for the little guy—the one Jesus called "the least of these."

The little guy I'm talking about was sitting on the floor in the aisle a couple rows in front of me. Although I couldn't hear the conversation between him and a security guard, I'm sure it went something like this:

"I'm sorry, sir, but I have to ask you to move. You can't sit on the floor. You're blocking the aisle."

"I'll scooch in so I'm out of the aisle."

"No, you have to find a seat. It's fire code."

"But there are no seats."

"There may be some on the third level. Or you can stand in the obstructed-view section over there."

"But I'll just . . . "

It was then that a man wearing a teal polo shirt volunteered his reserved seat for the little guy without one. Quicker than a smile and a gesture, the little guy was sitting on prime real estate with a view, and the other man was standing in the obstructed view section.

Although I didn't see him again until the farewell challenge, I couldn't help noticing him then, because he was the one delivering it. Sixty-five thousand men sat with their eyes riveted on Bill McCartney. But as impressive as his parting challenge was when everybody was watching, it seemed insignificant next to his gesture of kindness that only a few of us saw. His exchange with the little guy provided the real snapshot of his character.

What would a snapshot of your character look like? Perhaps the answer comes only when you have opportunity to help the little guy. As Jesus said: "The King will reply, 'I tell you the truth, whatever you did for one of the least of these brothers of mine, you did for me'" (Matt. 25:40).

I'd Rather Be in Hell

Once upon a time the king's best personal servant was walking in a dense forest near the palace. There he stumbled and fell down a hill. When he awakened, he looked around and found at his feet the proverbial magic bottle that, when rubbed, released a genie.

The genie said, "Your finding this bottle was no accident. You've worked hard all your life. So you may receive one wish. But make it carefully, because you can have only one."

The man replied, "All my life I have been in positions requiring that I serve others. In fact, I'm known as 'The Servant of the Kingdom.' In the future I want people to wait on me and serve me. Yes, that's it. I want the tables turned. I want servants to do everything for me."

Sure enough, when the man returned to the castle, the door was opened for him. His food was cooked, his meals were served, his dishes washed, his clothes cared for by others.

The palace staff would not allow him to perform his usual work—everything was done for him. For the first month the newness of the experience amused him. The second month it became irritating. During the third month it became unbearable.

So the man returned to the forest and searched until he found the genie again. He said, "I've discovered that having people wait on me isn't as pleasant as I'd thought. I'd like to return to my original station and once again be 'The Servant of the Kingdom.'"

The genie replied, "I'm sorry, but I can't help you. I had the power to grant only one wish."

"But you don't understand. I want to serve people. I found it far more rewarding to do things for others than to have all those things done for me." The genie just shook his head.

The man begged, "But you must help me. I'd rather be in hell than not be able to serve others."

The genie said sorrowfully, "Where do you think you have been, my friend, for the past 90 days?"*

"Whoever serves me must follow me. Then my servant will be with me everywhere I am. My Father will honor anyone who serves me"
(John 12:26, EB).

---

* A french fable, retold by Cavett Robert.

How Would You Like to Live Longer?

How would you like to live longer? Suppose I assured you that you could improve your odds of longevity by 250 percent; would you be interested? Suppose it wouldn't require changing your diet to oat bran and tree bark. Further, suppose that you wouldn't have to change your exercise program. You wouldn't need to jog 10 miles a day in those horrid Lycra shorts.

Still interested?

James House of the University of Michigan claims you can greatly increase your odds of living longer. How? According to his research, you will live longer if you volunteer to help others. House says, "We are used to the doctor saying, 'Take two aspirins and see me in the morning.' But in the future, he or she may say, 'Go do something to help other people and come see me in a week.'

"A 10-year study indicates that those people who do not volunteer, who do not help others, are 2.5 times more likely to die than those people who regularly help others."

Helping others strengthens you not only physically but spiritually as well. To Christians, service is not a nice suggestion—it's the heartbeat of faith. The apostle John put it like this: "Let us not love with words or tongue but with actions and in truth" (1 John 3:18).

To merely talk of being a Christian is as useless as a pitcher of warm spit. We show our Christianity by serving.

A smelly old tramp was looking for a handout one day in a picturesque English village. Hungry almost to the point of fainting, he stopped by a pub bearing the classic name Inn of St. George and the Dragon.

"Please, ma'am, could you spare me a bite to eat?" he asked the woman who answered his knock at the kitchen door.

"A bite to eat?" she growled. "For a sorry, no-good bum, a foul-smelling beggar? Not on your life," she snapped as she almost slammed the door on his hand.

Halfway down the lane the tramp stopped, turned around, and eyed the words "St. George and the Dragon." Returning, he knocked again.

"Now what do you want?" the woman asked angrily.

"Well, ma'am, if Saint George is in, may I speak to him this time?"

It's one thing to advertise being a saint; it's another thing to show it.

How Would You Like to Die?

It was like skinny-dipping in the Arctic. Jogging by Auburn Elementary School, I staggered like a drunk on ice. I had set out to exercise my body but exercised my spiritual gift instead—by eavesdropping.

Straining to hear above the biting wind, I slowed my gait as I approached the crosswalk. "Good morning, Jessica," the boy greeted a girl. Decorated with a reflective vest four sizes too big, he valiantly waved his fluorescent orange flag to assure her safe passage.

Sliding by him, the girl replied, "Hey, Matthew. How are you?"

"I'm about to freeze to death."

It was her response that I loved most. I raced home to preserve her wisdom in my journal.

"Well," she said, "if you do freeze to death, at least you'd die in the service!"

That's how I'd like to die. How about you? Can you think of a better way to die than "in the service"?

I can't.

Yep, that's the way I want to go: escorting a kid across the intersection, serenading the shut-ins, roofing a homeless shelter, listening to a hurting friend, buying groceries for an Alzheimer's patient, or raking leaves for grandma. In my mind the greatest tribute that anyone could share at my funeral would be that I lived to serve.

????'s to Ponder

What do you want to be remembered for? What do you hope your friends say about you at your funeral? What do you hope your enemies say? What can you do today to shape your life around what matters most? Will you be able to look back over your life and echo the parting words of the apostle Paul: "For I am already being poured out like a drink offering, and the time has come for my departure. I have fought the good fight, I have finished the race, I have kept the faith" (2 Tim. 4:6, 7)?

Perspectives on Service

"There are a lot of Christians who are doing nothing. But there are no Christians who have nothing to do."—*Author Unknown.*

"Command those who are rich in this present world not to be arrogant nor to put their hope in wealth, which is so uncertain, but to put their hope in God, who richly provides us with everything for our enjoyment. Command them to do good, to be rich in good deeds, and to be generous and willing to share. In this way they will lay up treasure for themselves as a firm foundation for the coming age, so that they may take hold of the life that is truly life."—1 Timothy 6:17-19.

A little fellow in the ghetto was teased by one who said, "If God loves you, why doesn't He take care of you? Why doesn't God tell someone to bring you shoes and a warm coat and better food?" The little lad thought for a moment, then said, "I guess He does tell somebody, but somebody forgets."

"Love, to be real, must cost. It must hurt. It must empty us of self."—Mother Teresa.

I asked, "Why doesn't somebody do something?" Then I realized I am somebody.

John Henry Jowett told about a small village in which an elderly woman died. She perished penniless, unedu-cated, unsophisticated, but during her lifetime her selfless service had made a tremendous impact for Christ. On her tombstone they chiseled the words "She did what she couldn't."

That can be the epitaph for every Christian who will allow Christ to live through us: He can do through us what we can never do ourselves.

"When it comes to loving the unlovable, easy doesn't do it."—S. Rickly Christian.

A nineteenth-century painting shows a long row of beggars waiting in a soup line. They are all ragged and sleazy looking. But around the head of one, barely perceptible, is a halo. One of them is Christ! You may see no halo around the heads of your brothers and sisters in need, yet to serve them is to serve Christ, for the King is hidden in them.

"He who oppresses the poor shows contempt for their Maker, but whoever is kind to the needy honors God."—Proverbs 14:31.

"There is no better exercise for the heart than reaching down and lifting people up."—John Andrew Holmer.

"Our Lord does not care so much for the importance of our works as for the love with which they are done."—Teresa of Avila.

Got a Story?

If you would like to send the author your comments or interesting stories, write:

Karl Haffner
1301 South Baltimore
Tacoma, WA 98465 U.S.A.

Or send your messages via CompuServe: E-mail address, 74532,123

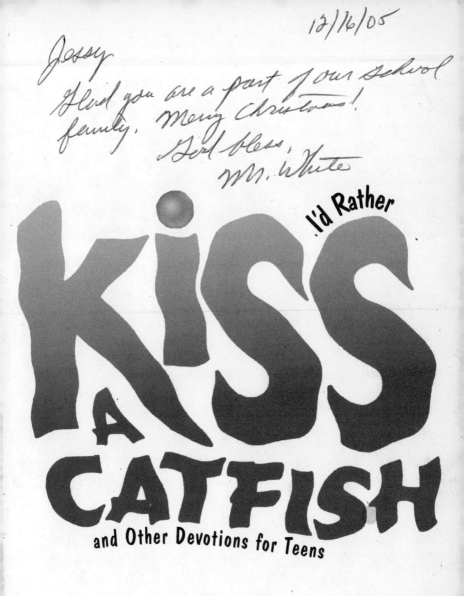

12/16/05

Jessy
Glad you are a part of our school family. Merry Christmas!
God bless,
M. White

Kiss
I'd Rather!
a
CATFISH
and Other Devotions for Teens